Cambridge Elements ≡

Elements in Ancient East Asia
edited by
Erica Fox Brindley
Pennsylvania State University
Rowan Kimon Flad
Harvard Unive̶̶̶̶

T0328187

THE METHODS AND ETHICS OF RESEARCHING UNPROVENIENCED ARTIFACTS FROM EAST ASIA

Christopher J. Foster
Independent Scholar

Glenda Chao
Ursinus College

Mercedes Valmisa
Gettysburg College

CAMBRIDGE
UNIVERSITY PRESS

Shaftesbury Road, Cambridge CB2 8EA, United Kingdom

One Liberty Plaza, 20th Floor, New York, NY 10006, USA

477 Williamstown Road, Port Melbourne, VIC 3207, Australia

314–321, 3rd Floor, Plot 3, Splendor Forum, Jasola District Centre, New Delhi – 110025, India

103 Penang Road, #05–06/07, Visioncrest Commercial, Singapore 238467

Cambridge University Press is part of Cambridge University Press & Assessment, a department of the University of Cambridge.

We share the University's mission to contribute to society through the pursuit of education, learning and research at the highest international levels of excellence.

www.cambridge.org
Information on this title: www.cambridge.org/9781009475723

DOI: 10.1017/9781009106771

First published 2024

A catalogue record for this publication is available from the British Library

ISBN 978-1-009-47572-3 Hardback
ISBN 978-1-009-10746-4 Paperback
ISSN 2632-7325 (online)
ISSN 2632-7317 (print)

The Methods and Ethics of Researching Unprovenienced Artifacts from East Asia

Elements in Ancient East Asia

DOI: 10.1017/9781009106771
First published online: January 2024

Christopher J. Foster
Independent Scholar

Glenda Chao
Ursinus College

Mercedes Valmisa
Gettysburg College

Author for correspondence: Glenda Chao, gchao@ursinus.edu

Abstract: The immense outpouring of archaeological discoveries this past century has shed new light on ancient East Asia, and China in particular. Yet, in concert with this development, another, more troubling trend has likewise gained momentum: the looting of cultural heritage and the sale of unprovenienced antiquities. Scholars face difficult questions, from the ethics of working with objects of unknown provenance, to the methodological problems inherent in their research. The goal of this Element is to encourage scholars to critically examine their relationships with their sources and reflect on the impact of their research. The three sections in this Element present a range of disciplinary perspectives, focusing on systemic issues and the nuances of method versus ethics, with a case study of the so-called Han board manuscripts given as a specific illustration. This title is also available as Open Access on Cambridge Core.

Keywords: unprovenienced artifacts, early China, ethics, methods, looting

ISBNs: 9781009475723 (HB), 9781009107464 (PB), 9781009106771 (OC)
ISSNs: 2632-7325 (online), 2632-7317 (print)

Contents

1 To Research or Ignore the So-Called Han Board Manuscripts: An Opinion (Christopher J. Foster)

In 2019, Zhonghua shuju 中華書局 published a cache of wooden-board manuscripts identified as from the Han period (hereafter the "Han board MSS") and currently in the possession of an anonymous party. The volume, *Xinjian Han du Cang Jie pian Shi pian jiaoshi* 新見漢牘蒼頡篇史篇校釋 by Liu Huan 劉桓 (hereafter *Xinjian Han du*), contains what could be the longest witness of an important scribal primer, the *Cang Jie pian* 蒼頡篇, two previously unknown primers, and a short poem.[1] These manuscripts could prove instrumental for the study of scribal training in ancient China at a crucial moment in the development of textual practices during the early imperial era. Yet the Han board MSS will forever be tainted by one sad fact: they are of uncertain provenance. Questions will always linger over whether these manuscripts are genuine. Even if they are genuine, their archaeological contexts, which could reveal much more about who possessed these texts and why, have been lost. The Han board MSS do not represent an isolated case. Institutions including the Shanghai Museum (in 1994), Tsinghua University (in 2008), Peking University (in 2009), and Anhui University (in 2019) have also acquired large caches of important early Chinese manuscripts.[2] It has gotten to the point where almost every scholar who works on early China, regardless of their specialization, now faces the difficult questions of if and how to use such sources for research. This is not a problem unique to the field of early China either, but it threatens Chinese antiquities generally,[3] and

---

[1] Liu Huan 劉桓, *Xinjian Han du Cang Jie pian Shi pian jiaoshi* 新見漢牘蒼頡篇史篇校釋 (Beijing: Zhonghua, 2019); Christopher J. Foster, "Further Considerations for the Authentication of the Peking University *Cang Jie pian*: With Brief Digression on the So-Called 'Han Board' Witness," *Early China* 44 (2021), 419–464.

[2] Ma Chengyuan 馬承源, ed., Shanghai bowuguan cang Zhanguo Chu zhushu 上海博物館藏戰國楚竹書. 9 vols. (Shanghai: Shanghai guji, 2001–12); Qinghua daxue chutu wenxian yanjiu yu baohu zhongxin 清華大學出土文獻研究與保護中心, Li Xueqin 李學勤 (vols. 1.8), Huang Dekuan 黃德寬 (vols.9–12), eds., *Qinghua daxue cang Zhanguo zhujian* 清華大學藏戰國竹簡. 12 vols. (Shanghai: Zhonghua shuju, 2010–22); Beijing daxue chutu wenxian yanjiusuo 北京大學出土文獻研究所, ed., *Beijing daxue cang Xi Han zhushu* 北京大學藏西漢竹書. 5 vols. (Shanghai: Shanghai guji, 2012–15); and Anhui daxue Han zi fazhan yu yingyong yanjiu zhongxin 安徽大學漢字發展與應用研究中心, Huang Dekuan 黃德寬, and Xu Zaiguo 徐在國, eds., *Anhui daxue cang Zhanguo zhujian* 安徽大學藏戰國竹簡. 2 vols. (Shanghai: Zhonghua shuju, 2019–22). For a recent survey of newly discovered manuscripts, including those acquired from the antiquities markets, see Olivier Venture, "Recently Excavated Inscriptions and Manuscripts (2008–2018)," *Early China* 44 (2021), 493–546.

[3] For surveys of looting in China and the illicit trade in Chinese antiquities, see He Shuzhong, "Illicit Excavation in Contemporary China," in Neil Brodie, Jennifer Doole, and Colin Renfrew, eds., *Trade in Illicit Antiquities: The Destruction of the World's Archaeological Heritage* (Cambridge: McDonald Institute for Archaeological Research, 2001), pp. 19–24; and Robert E. Murowchick, "'Despoiled of the Garments of Her Civilization': Problems and Progress in Archaeological Heritage Management in China," in Anne P. Underhill, ed., *A Companion to Chinese Archaeology* (Malden, MA: John Wiley/Blackwell, 2013), pp. 13–34.

indeed Asian cultural heritage more broadly conceived, especially from other source nations such as Cambodia or Thailand.[4]

In recent articles, Paul Goldin articulated some of the ethical concerns inherent to working with unprovenanced bamboo strips, emphasizing how scholarly research on such manuscripts lends expertise and authentication that increase the prestige and value of these pieces. This is a possible stimulus to the illicit antiquities market that incentivizes looting and thereby the further destruction of cultural heritage, what I will refer to here as the "market catalyst critique."[5] In response to Goldin's concerns, I have offered a brief defense of the study of caches like the Peking University Han strips, voicing a "salvage principle."[6] My argument is that these manuscripts also constitute important cultural heritage and that their protection and study should be prioritized over the unspecified losses to future looting inspired by this scholarship. The publication of the Han board MSS presents an opportunity to revisit this conversation. The following takes the Han board MSS as a case study through which to reflect on the dilemma of working with unprovenanced objects. It seeks to extend and refine the terms of the discourse and to model questions for researchers to ask. The Han board MSS are treated in light of both the "market catalyst critique" and the "salvage principle" in turn, giving arguments in support of each position, but then also pressing their commitments to extremes, challenging both their theoretical basis and their practicality.

Preliminaries: Unprovenanced Objects, Looted Artifacts, and the Problem of Authority

Before discussing the Han board MSS case study, a few preliminary comments are warranted concerning terminology and the problem of looting. I will begin with the most basic question: what actually counts as a "looted" artifact? Recent discussions on the professional ethics of working with looted artifacts in the early

---

[4] Colin Renfrew, *Loot, Legitimacy, and Ownership* (London: Gerald Duckworth & Company, 2000), pp. 58–60; Christine Alder, Duncan Chappell, and Kenneth Polk, "Perspectives on the Organisation and Control of the Illicit Traffic in Antiquities in South East Asia," paper presented at Organised Crime in Art and Antiquities, Courmayeur Mont Blanc, Italy, December 12–14, 2009, pp. 119–144. https://ro.uow.edu.au/lawpapers/76.

[5] See Paul R. Goldin, "Heng Xian and the Problem of Studying Looted Artifacts," *Dao* 12.2 (2013), 152–160; and "The Problem of Looted Artifacts in Chinese Studies: A Rejoinder to Critics," *Dao* 22.1 (2023), 145–151. See also, more generally, Renfrew, *Loot, Legitimacy, and Ownership*, 74–77, on the role of academics.

[6] Christopher J. Foster, "Introduction to the Peking University Han Bamboo Strips: On the Authentication and Study of Purchased Manuscripts," *Early China* 40 (2017), 167–239. For discussion of the merits and problems of this argument based on other case studies, see the survey in Alison Wylie, "Ethical Dilemmas in Archaeological Practice: Looting, Repatriation, Stewardship, and the (Trans)formation of Disciplinary Identity," *Perspectives on Science* 4.2 (1996), 154–194 (at 167–180), from which I borrow "salvage principle."

China field have focused predominantly on the bamboo-strip manuscripts acquired by the aforementioned institutions.[7] A point that may be obvious, but still deserves reiteration, is that scholarship on early China has long incorporated unprovenanced objects of other types too, including most prominently oracle bones and bronze vessels, and continues to do so.[8] One example of particular import – if genuine – is the X Gong *xu* (rendered variously as Bin or Sui Gong *xu* 豳/遂公盨) vessel the Poly Art Museum acquired in 2002.[9] The unprovenanced vessel bears an unique inscription, which both mentions the cultural hero Yu 禹 and employs language reminiscent of the *Shangshu* 尚書. Since its publication, the X Gong *xu* vessel has inspired an international conference in its honor (Dartmouth College, 2003),[10] been featured in numerous publications, and is included in a source book of ancient Chinese bronze inscriptions translated into English.[11] Discussions on professional ethics apply equally to the use of vessels like the X Gong *xu*, or any other unprovenanced object.

Terms like "unprovenanced," "unprovenienced," or "purchased" – the latter of which I adopted in my previous article but have since discarded – are useful descriptors for such artifacts because they acknowledge that the given piece

---

[7] Goldin, "Heng Xian" and "The Problem"; Foster, "Introduction"; Martin Kern, "'Xi Shuai' 蟋蟀 ('Cricket') and Its Consequences: Issues in Early Chinese Poetry and Textual Studies," *Early China* 42 (2019), 39–74; Michael Friedrich, "Producing and Identifying Forgeries of Chinese Manuscripts," in Cécile Michel and Michael Friedrich, eds., *Fakes and Forgeries of Written Artefacts from Ancient Mesopotamia to Modern China* (Berlin: Walter de Gruyter, 2020), pp. 291–336; Adam Smith and Maddalena Poli, "Establishing the Text of the *Odes*: The Anhui University Bamboo Manuscript," *Bulletin of the School of Oriental and African Studies* 84.3 (2021), 515–557 (at 519–520); Edward L. Shaughnessy, "General Preface II (A Note on the Authenticity of the Tsinghua Manuscripts and the Ethics of Preserving Looted Cultural Artifacts)," in Edward L. Shaughnessy, ed., The Tsinghua University Warring States Bamboo Manuscripts: Studies and Translations 1: The *Yi Zhou Shu* and Pseudo-*Yi Zhou Shu* Chapters (Beijing: Qinghua daxue chubanshe, 2023), pp. 8–21; and in passim elsewhere – for example, Yuri Pines, Zhou History Unearthed: The Bamboo Manuscript *Xinian* and Early Chinese Historiography (New York: Columbia University Press, 2020), pp. 43–44; Lothar von Falkenhausen, "Review of Yuri Pines, *Zhou History Unearthed*," *Journal of Chinese Studies* (*Zhongguo wenhua yanjiusuo xuebao* 中國文化研究所學報) 73 (2021), 263–267 (at 266–267).

[8] These practices trace back even to antiquity itself – for instance, with Song- through Qing-period antiquarian catalogs of bronze vessels and their inscriptions. Although distant from modern looting networks and market dynamics (Goldin, "The Problem," 146, note 2), these practices still constitute a foundational background to the study of early China, as Glenda Chao emphasizes in Section 2.

[9] Baoli yishu bowuguan 保利藝術博物館, ed., *X Gong Xu: Da Yu Zhishui yu Wei Zheng yi de* 豳龘火公盨——大禹治水與爲政以德 (Beijing: Xianzhuang, 2002); with articles by Li Xueqin 李學勤, Qiu Xigui 裘錫圭, Zhu Fenghan 朱鳳瀚, and Li Ling 李零 also in *Zhongguo lishi wenwu* 中國歷史文物 2002.6.

[10] Xing Wen 邢文, ed., *The X Gong Xu* 豳龘火公盨: *A Report and Papers from the Dartmouth Workshop*, in *International Research on Bamboo and Silk Documents Newsletter*, special issue (2003).

[11] Constance A. Cook and Paul R. Goldin, eds., *A Source Book of Ancient Chinese Bronze Inscriptions* (Berkeley, CA: Society for the Study of Early China, 2020 [2016]), pp. 195–196.

may not be looted, but potentially a forgery instead.[12] Not all "unprovenanced" objects are looted. Similarly, when it comes to a "looted" artifact, it would be imprecise to limit our focus to merely the absence of details on provenance (as implied by "unprovenanced"), or the fact that it was acquired from an antiquities market (as implied by "purchased"). That is to say, not all potentially "looted" artifacts are unprovenanced or purchased. The designation of an act as looting, rather, depends on a *transgression of authority* in an artifact's discovery and/or possession. Any disturbance of past material remains, even if done following the most cautious scientific archaeological methods, is inevitably destructive and entails a degree of loss. The question really is who controls access to cultural heritage, decides what merits protection and what loss is tolerable, and then sanctifies best practices for that access and protection. Answers to these questions are open to challenge, as examined further in Section 2 by Glenda Chao and Section 3 by Mercedes Valmisa.

Consider, for instance, the mixed legacy of Aurel Stein. His expeditions to Central Asia in the early twentieth century and recovery of numerous manuscripts – most now held in the British Library – won him knighthood in the British Empire, as well as scholarly accolades, a few explicitly awarded for his contributions to archaeology.[13] Stein sought permits for his fieldwork, kept detailed records of his finds, for which provenance is meticulously documented, and went to great lengths to distance his research from the exploits of mere "treasure hunters."[14] Yet numerous Chinese intellectuals, both at the time and

---

[12] For the difference between "provenance" and "provenience," see Goldin, "Heng Xian," 156, note 6. In this section, I have opted for "unprovenanced" as a general qualifier, even though this practice conflicts with Chao and Valmisa's adoption of "unprovenienced," which also appears in the title of our Element. I feel that the emphasis in "provenance" on history of ownership is more expansive than the focus of "provenience" on point of origin, making it better suited for describing the nature of these objects in the current debate. On discarding "purchased" for "unprovenanced," see Foster, "Further Considerations," 421.

[13] Sarah Strong and Helen Wang, "Sir Aurel Stein's Medals at the Royal Geographical Society," in Helen Wang, ed., *Sir Aurel Stein, Colleagues and Collections*. British Museum Research Publication Number 184 (London: British Museum, 2012), pp. 1–10. The *Sir Aurel Stein, Colleagues and Collections* volume may be found online in the British Museum Research Publications full list at www.britishmuseum.org/research/publications/research-publications-series.

[14] "The thought of the grave risks with which nature and, still more, human activity threaten all these relics of antiquity, was ever present to my mind, and formed an urgent incentive to unwearied exertion, however trying the conditions of work might be ... I could not fail to be impressed by the warnings of impending destruction through the hand of man ... there were the evidence traces of the mischief done by Khotan 'treasure-seekers' at the more accessible sites, and also, alas! a vivid remembrance of the irretrievable loss which the study of Indian art and antiquities has suffered through 'irresponsible digging' carried on until recent years by, and for, amateur collectors among the ruined Buddhist shrines of the North-West Frontier of India." M. Aurel Stein, *Sand-Buried Ruins of Khotan: Personal Narrative of a Journey of Archaeological and Geographical Exploration in Chinese Turkestan* (London: Hurst and Blackett, 1904), "Introduction," p. xx.

still today, characterize Stein as a looter who plundered cultural relics from the region.[15] There are many factors behind these starkly divergent characterizations of Stein and his work, but what I wish to highlight here is how ambiguity over *authority* created a space for this controversy. During Stein's expeditions, scientific archaeology was still in its infancy in China; political instability unsettled the region and indeed the world; international agreements over the appropriate stewardship of cultural heritage did not yet exist; and, crucially, a newfound Chinese nationalism came into conflict with European and Japanese imperialism, a point Chao also emphasizes.[16]

Of course, the situation today is dramatically different. Archaeology is a well-defined discipline in the People's Republic of China (PRC), with institutional structure and professional guidelines.[17] The PRC government has passed strict laws aimed at the protection of cultural heritage – for example, the Law of People's Republic of China on the Protection of Cultural Relics (中華人民共和國文物保護法), last amended in 2007.[18] Treaties such as the 1970 United

---

[15] For example, Liu Guozhong 劉國忠 begins his survey of discoveries of bamboo and silk manuscripts by writing that, in the late nineteenth and early twentieth centuries, "a few foreign adventurers, in the name of exploration, entered China's Xinjiang, Gansu and Inner Mongolia provinces, and conducted so-called expeditions, recklessly looting local graves and archaeological sites, pillaging cultural relics" (*Zoujin Qinghua jian* 走近清華簡 [Beijing: Gaodeng jiaoyu, 2011], pp. 21–22); compare to the English translation by Christopher J. Foster and William N. French, which softens the tones of these lines (*Introduction to the Tsinghua Bamboo-Strip Manuscripts* [Leiden: Brill, 2015], p. 27). Certain of Stein's actions do demonstrate a distinct disregard for local authorities. Consider his admission, in the field notes for a visit to Niya in January 1931, of distracting his guards in order to allow hired hands to survey the site undeterred: "So I decided to let Abdul Gh. return here [N.XIV] with three men of our own party ... Abdul Gh. with three men started before day break for clearing of refuse at N.XIV. Self spent day in camp with packing of miscell. finds & writing up diary, thus keeping our 'guards' from investigation" (MS. Stein 224, Weston Library, Oxford, 318 [January 20 and 21, 1931]).

[16] On the history of cultural heritage legislation and protection in China, see the brief surveys in Murowchick, "'Despoiled,'" 15–19, and in Jian Li, Hui Fang, and Anne P. Underhill, "The History of Perception and Protection of Cultural Heritage in China," in Anne P. Underhill and Lucy C. Salazar, eds., *Finding Solutions for Protecting and Sharing Archaeological Heritage Resources* (New York: Springer, 2015), pp. 1–16. On the complex entanglement of Western imperialism and Chinese nationalism and the "thin line" between them, examined through the lens of Aurel Stein's reception in China, see Justin Jacobs, "Confronting Indiana Jones: Chinese Nationalism, Historical Imperialism, and the Criminalization of Aurel Stein and the Raiders of Dunhuang, 1899–1944," in Sherman Cochran and Paul Pickowicz, eds., *China on the Margins* (Ithaca, NY: Cornell East Asia Program, 2010), pp. 65–90; and "Nationalist China's 'Great Game': Leveraging Foreign Explorers in Xinjiang, 1927–1935," *Journal of Asian Studies* 73.1 (2014), 43–64.

[17] See, for instance, Guojia wenwu ju 國家文物局, *Tianye kaogu gongzuo guicheng* 田野考古工作規程 (Beijing: Wenwu chubanshe, 2009).

[18] Text of the law is accessible online at the National People's Congress of the People's Republic of China website: www.npc.gov.cn/wxzl/gongbao/2015-08/10/content_1942927.htm. For discussion of this particular law (ca.1990s), its historical precedents, and other legislative and administrative features of PRC cultural heritage protection, see J. David Murphy, *Plunder and Preservation: Cultural Property Law and Practice in the People's Republic of China* (Oxford:

Nations Educational Scientific and Cultural Organization (UNESCO) Convention on the Means of Prohibiting and Preventing the Illicit Import, Export and Transfer of Ownership of Cultural Property and the 1995 International Institute for the Unification of Private Law (UNIDROIT) Convention on Stolen or Illegally Exported Cultural Objects provide additional guidelines for both domestic and international regulation of the antiquities trade.[19] For decades now, a dialogue has taken place over how to legally and ethically handle unprovenanced objects and combat the problem of looting, with the participation of archaeologists, museum curators, art collectors, learned societies, politicians, lawyers, and other stakeholders all across the world.[20] Clear authorities exist to whom one may appeal for direction on access to and the preservation of cultural heritage in China.

Ethical concerns might be raised to challenge these authorities, and conflicts between authorities likewise complicate assessments of what constitutes a "looted" artifact. A PRC law declares state ownership for all cultural relics remaining underground within its territory, with government permissions required before excavation and granted only to projects led by trained archaeologists. This prioritizes the scientific exploitation of past material remains as a public good, with archaeologists granted privileged access to cultural heritage. While safeguarding the scientific study of the past is undeniably an admirable goal, a risk remains both of mobilizing cultural heritage for nationalistic agendas and of disregarding nonarchaeological interests in shared cultural heritage.[21] Should local families in China have a right to decide if the ancestral graves of their village are excavated and, if so, what happens to the artifacts

---

Oxford University Press, 1995), pp. 76–142; for a critical piece on the shortcomings of the law and its later amendment, see Amanda K. Maus, "Safeguarding China's Cultural History: Proposed Amendments to the 2002 Law on the Protection of Cultural Relics," *Pacific Rim Law & Policy Journal* 18.2 (2009), 405–431. Background on the development of archaeology vis-à-vis cultural heritage protection in China is covered in Section 2, as well as in Murowchick, "'Despoiled,'" 14–22, and Li, Fang, and Underhill, "The History of Perception," 1–16.

[19] Text of the 1970 UNESCO Convention may be found on the UNESCO website: http://portal.unesco.org/en/ev.php-URL_ID=13039&URL_DO=DO_TOPIC&URL_SECTION=201.html; and the 1995 UNIDROIT Convention on the UNIDROIT website: www.unidroit.org/instruments/cultural-property/1995-convention.

[20] Patrick J. O'Keefe, *Trade in Antiquities: Reducing Destruction and Theft* (London: Archetype Publications and United Nations Educational Scientific and Cultural Organization, 1997) offers an accessible overview of these varied stakeholders, codes of conduct, and approaches we may adopt to combat looting. See also the useful database at https://archaeologicalethics.org.

[21] On the former, see Magnus Fiskesjö, "The Politics of Cultural Heritage," in You-tien Hsing and Ching Kwan Lee, eds., *Reclaiming Chinese Society: The New Social Activism* (Abingdon: Routledge, 2010), pp. 225–245. On the latter, see the comparable debate that has been held in North American archaeology, discussed in Wylie, "Ethical Dilemmas," 180–183. Note that the Society for American Archaeology initiated a task force in 2018 to review and update its principles of archaeological ethics. The statement of principles can be found at www.saa.org/career-practice/ethics-in-professional-archaeology.

recovered therein, by nature of being (or claiming to be) lineal descendants of the tomb occupants? Taking these questions seriously also begins to acknowledge the socioeconomic realities, raised by Chao and Valmisa, that compel locals to participate in looting for fiscal gain.

Governments are not always responsible custodians of cultural heritage either. A lack of enforcement or corruption can undermine well-intentioned laws. Certain PRC policies have elicited strong censure as well, including recently the treatment of Uyghur cultural heritage.[22] If a state's laws or activities are themselves deemed unjust, how might this impact treatment of artifacts procured in ways that subvert their authority? Indeed, critics of the acquisitions of bamboo strips by Peking University and other state-owned institutions might point to the PRC government's condoning of the purchases as unjustifiably incentivizing looting in the name of repatriation, and therefore a case of irresponsible custodianship of cultural heritage. Similar doubts may be cast on the authority of international agreements. The 1970 UNESCO Convention in essence grants amnesty to artifacts already on the market prior to the treaty, creating an – ultimately arbitrary – division of legitimate versus illegitimate antiquities for trade.[23] This arbitrary division may not be acceptable to everyone, complicating decisions about which artifacts merit boycott – for example, with debates concerning Stein's Dunhuang MSS, or over sales of the Old Summer Palace bronze zodiac heads, whose repatriation has generated great controversy (to be mentioned shortly).[24]

All of this, of course, begs yet another question, indeed the question that Chao uses to frame Section 2: who has the right to arbitrate which authorities are just and ethically merit compliance? There has been little public debate within China over the ethics of studying unprovenanced MSS. That research on these artifacts, including on the Han board MSS, has continued unabated by

---

[22] See Magnus Fiskesjö, "Cultural Genocide Is the New Genocide," *Pen/Opp*, May 5, 2020, www .penopp.org/articles/cultural-genocide-new-genocide; and "Bulldozing Culture: China's Systematic Destruction of Uyghur Heritage Reveals Genocidal Intent," *Cultural Property News*, June 23, 2021, https://culturalpropertynews.org/bulldozing-culture-chinas-systematic-destruction-of-uyghur-heritage-reveals-genocidal-intent; as well as his bibliography of academic articles and news reports related to "China's 're-education' / concentration camps in Xinjiang / East Turkistan, and the campaign of forced assimilation and genocide targeting Uyghurs, Kazakhs, etc." at Uyghur Human Rights Project: https://uhrp.org/bibliography.

[23] The arbitrary nature of the 1970 division is repeatedly mentioned in Renfrew, *Loot, Legitimacy, and Ownership*; see, for example, 11, 16, 22. I do not raise this as a critique of the 1970 UNESCO Convention, but rather to allow that, for certain stakeholders, there may be significant ethical reasons both to censure objects whose acquisitions fall before this point and also to condone those acquired afterward.

[24] For a study of the 1970 UNESCO Convention, its precedents, and its implementation, see Patrick J. O'Keefe, *Protecting Cultural Objects: Before and after 1970* (Crickadarn: Institute of Art and Law, 2017). Compare to Goldin "The Problem," 146, note 2, with the question in mind of how the "circumstances that still obtain today" bear political and economic ties to past acts.

Chinese scholars, may signal, on the whole, tacit acceptance of the salvage principle. This tacit acceptance may also be dictated by the political environment in China as well, where public dissent could be politically cast as unpatriotic.[25] On one hand, without the participation of Chinese stakeholders, one may rightfully disapprove moralizing statements on the stewardship of China's cultural heritage by non-Chinese parties based in European or American institutions, even if well intentioned, as echoes of hypocritical cultural imperialism.[26] On the other hand, this concession accepts the nationalistic narrative claiming all cultural heritage in China belongs to a Chinese nation-state; and if this political impetus is restricting the participation of Chinese stakeholders, then those outside of China are uniquely positioned to offer dissent.[27]

A Case against Studying the Han Board Manuscripts: Market Catalyst Critique

The Han board MSS are unprovenanced objects that, if genuine, were most likely looted. For the market catalyst critique, authentication is irrelevant. The major concern is whether or not the Han board MSS derived from the antiquities market, having been procured in a way that transgressed authorities (PRC, UNESCO, etc.) deemed just. Very little information is provided in *Xinjian Han du* about the circumstances surrounding any acquisition of the boards. The "Preface 前言" by Liu Huan only divulges: "In the autumn of 2009, I was fortunate enough to inspect a collection of wooden boards at a friend's residence in Beijing, and obtain photographs of these artifacts."[28] It is unknown if the Han board MSS were sold illicitly at market, but when facing an absence in details about how Liu's friend came into the possession of these boards, the ethical imperative falls on an assumption that they were sold illicitly.[29] Regardless, researching these objects signals a willingness to tolerate such ambiguity, which still legitimates working on unprovenanced objects that *could* participate in the illicit antiquities trade. To rephrase, then, best practice is to assume

---

[25] See Fiskesjö, "The Politics," 239. Dissenting voices can be found, in my experience, during casual conversation. Goldin offers a similar reflection in "The Problem," 3, note 5. See also note 62 of this Element for an article published in Chinese that does address the issue of working with unprovenanced manuscripts.

[26] Falkenhausen, "Review of Yuri Pines," 267; Dirk Meyer, "Antiquity Resurfaced," paper presented at Reading the Excavated Poetry (*Shijing*) from Early China: Perspectives from Paleography, Philology, Phonology, and Classical Exegesis, University of Notre Dame, October 26–28, 2018.

[27] Goldin, "The Problem," 147, note 5.

[28] Liu, *Xinjian Han du*, 1.

[29] Other possibilities exist for the possession of antiquities – for instance, having an object handed down as a family heirloom over the centuries. This specific example is extremely unlikely for this class of artifact, however, owing to difficulties in its preservation.

a transgression of just authority in cases that lack clear documentation to the contrary.[30]

In the case of the Han board MSS, the anonymity of the party in possession of the boards presents more pressing issues than those encountered in my prior discussions of the Peking University Han bamboo strips.[31] Peking University is a state-owned institution, which, in its acquisitions of bamboo strips, intervened in a domestic market to secure objects originating in China and pertinent to China's cultural heritage.[32] Although details surrounding the Peking University acquisitions remain opaque to the public, as a state-owned entity, presumably the university operated under the blessings of the PRC government as a form of repatriation.[33] Of course, as Goldin warns, repatriation still impacts the market for illicit antiquities.[34] Yet despite these complaints, care for the Peking University bamboo strips has been subjected transparently to PRC law thereafter: the acquisition was announced in the media, the data published or being published, the artifacts now conserved in a state-owned institution and, moreover, made accessible, to both researchers and the broader public.

The Han board MSS, however, are held privately. Crucially, this means that the current possessor of the Han board MSS is not transparently accountable for their stewardship of the objects, and thereby skirts direct oversight, whether under PRC law or international agreements, including, for instance, restrictions over resale of the boards on the illicit antiquities market. Whoever now possesses the Han board MSS is an individual (or individuals) who we must assume has (or have) directly and actively engaged in the illicit antiquities trade already.

---

[30] Renfrew, *Loot, Legitimacy, and Ownership*, 29.

[31] Foster, "Introduction"; Foster, "Further Considerations."

[32] The editors of the Peking University cache of Han strips describe the artifacts as "returning from overseas" (從海外回歸), likely a reference to Hong Kong, which is a known hub for the illicit antiquities trade in bamboo-strip manuscripts. The Shanghai Museum acquisition of manuscripts occurred prior to the British government's handover of Hong Kong administration to the PRC, but for later acquisitions, Hong Kong can be considered a domestic market, even while acknowledging its liminal political status as a special administrative region under "one country, two systems." The use of language such as "overseas," however, in these latter contexts, emphasizes the threat of "national treasures" (國寶) disappearing to foreign market nations, bolstering a mandate for repatriation. Note also Ozawa Kenji's 小沢賢二 claim that the Peking University Han strips were brought to Beijing by an antique dealer in the latter half of 2008: Asano Yūichi 浅野裕一 and Ozawa Kenji 小沢賢二, *Sekkōdai saden shingikō* 浙江大左伝真偽考 (Tokyo: Kyūkoshoin, 2013), 2 (291). The implication is that university affiliates did not actually bring the artifacts into Mainland China.

[33] Comparison may be made to the similar acquisition by Tsinghua University, for which Liu Guozhong details the involvement of party members; see Liu, *Zoujin Qinghua jian*, 51–54. For a defense of Tsinghua acquisition, as both abiding by international conventions and falling under the purview of PRC authority, see Shaughnessy, "General Preface II."

[34] Goldin, "Heng Xian," 158; Goldin, "The Problem," 146. Though see also Renfrew, *Loot, Legitimacy, and Ownership*, 45, on the role repatriation can play in suppressing the market. Recall also Hong Kong's ambivalent status.

Scholarship on the objects they possess could lead to their personal enrichment, such as by advertising the boards' value for potential resale, emboldening their continued participation on the market. In other words, the Han board MSS present an especially precarious case, as the untrustworthy status of the boards' current caretaker, the lack of transparency in that party's future activities, and the possible continued circulation of the cultural heritage in their keep amplifies the potential negative impact of scholarship on the Han board MSS.[35]

Furthermore, the anonymity of the party in possession of the Han board MSS makes it difficult, if not impossible, for researchers to access the pieces for study or proper authentication. Control over data about the Han board MSS by an untrustworthy caretaker potentially biases scholarship on them. Moreover, by nature of being in a private collection, the Han board MSS are withdrawn from the realm of shared cultural heritage and cannot be enjoyed by the broader public. No appeal can be made to repatriation as a mitigating factor justifying the loss rendered by its negative market impact. Without the oversights established by PRC law or international agreements, there are no mandates for responsible stewardship of the Han board MSS, which, beyond merely the possibility of resale, also includes meeting proper standards for conservation, threatening the artifacts' preservation. In light of this, and here responding to the salvage principle, the Han board MSS offer tenuous value as cultural heritage, owing to the difficulties faced in their authentication, their being withdrawn from public audiences, and their impermanence threatened through uncertain preservation. These are all substantial reasons to dissuade scholars from working with the Han board MSS, beyond those already discussed for collections acquired by state-owned institutions.[36]

For scholars who oppose studying the Han board MSS, the question then is how to act upon their convictions. A minimal approach is to avoid mention of unprovenanced objects or looted artifacts in print, a form of self-censorship.[37] If the objective is to not advertise these sources, then it follows that indirect mention of the objects should be avoided as well, which is to say, refraining from citing secondary scholarship that uses these sources, in whole or in part, or, taken to an even greater extreme, secondary scholarship drawing from *yet other* studies that utilize these sources, and so forth ad infinitum. Otherwise, one is building upon insights and arguments derived from the unprovenanced objects

---

[35] These are the main differences, in regard to market impact, that separate collection by a private party from the institutional acquisitions, who also actively participated in the illicit antiquities trade and stand to benefit from scholarship on their collections – for instance, by garnering prestige.

[36] For the prior discussion on acquisitions by state-owned institutions, see Foster, "Introduction," 232–239.

[37] Goldin, "Heng Xian," 158; Goldin, "The Problem," 146.

or looted artifacts. But as Michael Friedrich (in discussion with Ondřej Škrabal) has recently warned, "there is little chance any more of disentangling the results obtained from genuine finds and dubious evidence."[38] Unprovenanced objects have become so thoroughly integrated into secondary scholarship on early China, untangling their influence is now largely futile at a practical level.[39]

The qualification "in print" is important as well, as it concedes that there is a lack of control over the audience for published statements, offering access to scholarship to a broader public, who potentially engage in the illicit antiquities trade. There are certain audiences, however, with whom it might be beneficial to reference unprovenanced artifacts: consultation with law enforcement or policymakers, students for teaching purposes, and scholarly exchange with other experts deemed responsible custodians of cultural heritage, for example, audiences who it may be hoped do not participate in the illicit antiquities market. Is it acceptable to discuss unprovenanced artifacts in more controlled and private settings, such as a classroom, or during a professional talk in a closed venue? A judicious decision must be made about how much information and which audiences are deemed dangerous enough for censorship. One may argue that even this short Element unduly advertises the Han board MSS, merely by describing their content or giving a citation to where the data have been published. Furthermore, if discussion of unprovenanced artifacts is permissible only for certain audiences, an obligation arises to ensure participation is restricted to that targeted audience, which is not always feasible.

Another consideration is how individual researchers – the most limited of audiences – should manage their own access to data on unprovenanced objects. This bears less on the argument that working on the Han board MSS incentivizes looting, but rather concerns transparency in scholarship. For those scholars convinced by the market catalyst critique, does personal reading of the Han board MSS risk biasing their knowledge in ways that may then, knowingly or not, change how they view other data in the field?[40] For example, the Han board *Cang Jie pian* includes explicit numbering on the boards, partially confirming prior reconstructions of chapters and chapter order, while also providing a more complete picture.[41] Having seen this manuscript, even if a scholar excises all references to the Han board witness in print, their frame of reference for the *Cang Jie pian* has been fundamentally altered. Should that frame of reference

---

[38] Friedrich, "Producing and Identifying," 330.
[39] These complications will impede those who pursue more aggressive approaches in censorship and protest as well, outlined later in this Element.
[40] Compare Goldin, "The Problem," 146.
[41] This is specifically for the Village Teachers edition of the text. See Foster, "Further Considerations," 455, note 91.

influence their interpretation of the text, even if only in subtle ways, then the lack of citations to the Han board MSS muddles their scholarship for uninitiated readers.[42]

These questions pertain mostly to individual choices on how best to conduct or present our own research in the form of self-censorship. Already, however, these choices begin to potentially impede upon the open scholarship of others, such as denying students access to developments in the field. Even more aggressive approaches could be advocated to prevent the engagement of other scholars with unprovenanced objects as well. This includes, at the level of individual researchers, refraining from citing other scholars' work that directly engages with unprovenanced artifacts, thereby limiting their audience; or, more dramatically, censoring *all work* of such scholars as a form of protest; refusing to accept money from funding bodies that have supported research on unprovenanced objects previously; and not affiliating with presses and journals who publish data and studies on such objects. Institutionally, as Goldin notes, many publishers in other fields have policies in place that actively censor pieces featuring unprovenanced artifacts, and it appears that similar thinking has begun to take root for some publishers of early China monographs as well.[43] Other forms of institutional boycott may include, for example, funding bodies refusing to issue grants for projects featuring unprovenanced objects; or universities not hiring candidates based on prior and/or planned future research on them.

These more aggressive forms of protest take seriously an understanding that, to be effective, silencing scholarship on unprovenanced or looted artifacts should aspire to be universal. It does little good for a handful of scholars to cease publishing on unprovenanced objects or looted artifacts, only to have the rest of the field continue to discuss them widely and advertise their value.[44] Here we may press the market catalyst theory to another extreme. The study of *any* bamboo-strip and wood-board manuscript, including scientifically excavated specimens, advertises the value of this class of artifact.[45] Though this

---

[42] Conversely, turning a blind eye to data from unprovenanced manuscripts – if genuine – risks corrupting the production of knowledge should they prove that narratives built upon the more limited corpus of data from transmitted texts or scientifically documented artifacts are misleading or incorrect. See later in this Element on using the chapter numbering to the *Cang Jie pian* found on the Han board MSS. This also presumes ignoring data from unprovenanced manuscripts remains feasible for the field, with the aforementioned doubts raised in Friedrich, "Producing and Identifying," 330.

[43] Pines, *Zhou History Unearthed*, 252, note 16.

[44] Foster, "Introduction," 235, note 189; see also Valmisa's section of this Element.

[45] Foster, "Introduction," 238; Smith and Poli, "Establishing," 520; Wylie, "Ethical Dilemmas," 172–174; and Alder et al., "Perspectives," 126: "Fads in the market also play a role, since events such as the Chinese Warriors exhibitions a few years ago tend to result in an increased demand

avoids the direct legitimation of unprovenanced objects or looted artifacts through providing "authentication and expertise" on those specimens, it still serves as a catalyst for the market and thereby can "aid and abet the sale of illicit antiquities."[46] Similarly, the licit trade in antiquities likewise establishes market values, from which the illicit trade may take a model. Should limits, therefore, be placed on the study or trade of any antiquities, as promoting the value of and legitimating ownership over the past?[47] This obviously leads to an untenable position that eschews study of the past in any form because it contributes to commercialization of the archaeological record. The point, however, is not to travel down this admittedly slippery slope. Rather, I wish to highlight that a compromise must be made between educating about the importance of China's past, and the risk that others will abuse the value this scholarship generates.

Furthermore, these more aggressive approaches also encroach upon basic principles of academic freedom and raise thorny issues over a conflict in "common goods," namely perceived best practices for the preservation of cultural heritage versus "the free search for truth and its free exposition."[48] Whatever benefits may be derived by marginalizing scholarship on unprovenanced objects and looted artifacts in these ways, by design, this marginalization alienates colleagues and promotes a divisive academic environment, rendering a lasting effect on our field. Even at the level of self-censorship, one risks an increasing disconnect between their work and those of peers who do choose to research unprovenanced objects or looted artifacts, with communication between them potentially untenable. For example, scholars researching the Han board *Cang Jie pian* may begin to refer to content by chapter numbers unknown to those ignoring this manuscript. Obviously, the more aggressive forms of protest more directly and forcefully antagonize colleagues and

---

for Chinese objects, with that demand falling off as the fad fades." Here Alder et al., in discussing the factors that shape the market for illicit antiquities, note a connection between museum exhibitions and rising market demand.

[46] Quotations here are in response to the call, echoed by Goldin, "Heng Xian," 158, as formulated in Renfrew, *Loot, Legitimacy, and Ownership*, 74: "That it is unethical and immoral to aid and abet the sale of illicit antiquities by offering authentication and expertise." Renfrew cites for this Karen Vitelli, ed., *Archaeological Ethics* (Walnut Creek, CA: Altamira Press, 1996).

[47] For a brief comment on the importance of maintaining a licit trade in antiquities, see Christine Alder and Kenneth Polk, "Stopping This Awful Business: The Illicit Traffic in Antiquities Examined As a Criminal Market," *Art, Antiquity and Law* 7.1 (2002), 35–53 (at 40–41).

[48] Citing from the American Association of University Professors "1940 Statement of Principles on Academic Freedom and Tenure," see www.aaup.org/report/1940-statement-principles-academic-freedom-and-tenure for the text and later interpretations. Ethical scholarship will entail certain limitations to the methods and scope of research, evident, for example, in the treatment of human and animal subjects. The appropriateness of these limitations, however, depends upon resolving conflicts in common goods, as faced in the scenario under discussion.

institutions. Are these tolerable growing pains that the field must go through in order to correct its course, for the sake of preserving China's cultural heritage? Or would they merely add additional stress upon a small field (which outside of China already has a tenuous existence) to chase an ultimately unattainable goal (i.e., universal boycott of working with unprovenanced objects and looted artifacts) for the sake of unproven and/or marginal impacts on the illicit antiquities trade? Sadly, those most vulnerable within this conflict of interests are graduate students and early career researchers, just starting out in the field, who do not have the safety net of tenure but must face restrictions over the sources they study, the grants they can apply for, the publishers who might accept their work, and potentially even the positions to which they may be hired.

A Case in Support of Studying the Han Board Manuscripts: Salvage Principle

Held by an untrustworthy party who is not subjected transparently to PRC law or international agreements, not easily accessible to researchers or a broader public audience as part of shared heritage, and kept under uncertain conservation conditions, the Han board MSS face a tenuous existence. Yet, if the salvage principle is taken seriously, it is precisely the precarious situation in which the boards are now found that makes it even more urgent to document and study their data. This research may ultimately be the *only* way to rescue their intellectual contributions and restore them to a shared cultural heritage, as the objects themselves may not survive or otherwise disappear entirely from scholarly view. Furthermore, Zhonghua shuju has already published photographs and transcriptions for the manuscripts, while a number of Chinese scholars have published their initial appraisals of the manuscripts' authenticity. Suppressing the circulation of these data now seems impracticable.[49] These are the main arguments in support of studying the Han board MSS: they are cultural heritage in great risk; study of them may offer the only means of salvaging this heritage; and suppressing the data is impracticable, even should suppression be deemed the best course of action.

For scholars who accept these reasons and wish to study the Han board MSS, a different series of questions and complications arise, especially concerning authentication. As stated, according to the market catalyst critique, authentication is irrelevant. According to the salvage principle, however, and concerning unprovenanced objects in particular, in order to justify intervention into the

---

[49] This justification highlights the question of whether *first-time* publication of privately acquired unprovenanced objects warrants special censure. It is this act, after all, that gives more widespread introduction to the existence and value of the objects.

illicit antiquities trade – in this case, by studying the Han board MSS, which presumedly were purchased via that market – it is vital to understand the nature of the cultural heritage being saved. Not knowing if the Han board MSS are indeed looted ancient artifacts or modern forgeries presents uncertainty that compromises their value for scholarship. Conducting research on the Han board MSS could in fact prove actively detrimental to the field of early China studies, beyond the incentivization of looting, should they be modern forgeries treated as ancient artifacts. This introduces false data that can perniciously influence interpretations given for other legitimate ancient artifacts. Let me emphasize, however, that even if the Han board MSS are demonstrated to be modern forgeries, they still represent meaningful cultural heritage, just of a different sort: they could tell scholars much, for instance, about contemporary imaginations of early China.

Authentication must be prioritized when treating unprovenanced objects. Yet practical limitations befall those who study unprovenanced objects and consequently face this imperative to authenticate. The three pillars of authentication are provenance tracing, connoisseurship, and scientific testing.[50] With institutional collections like that of Peking University, provenance tracing is hindered by the absence of details over how the manuscripts were acquired. As for connoisseurship, not all researchers are able to handle strips personally; moreover, access to the unprovenanced objects themselves may be restricted by the institutions or logistically inconvenient (especially for those based outside of China).[51] Finally, with scientific testing, decisions over if and how to conduct tests like radiocarbon dating are made by the institutions holding the pieces and must take into account costs and the artifacts' welfare. Thus obstacles exist for researchers in each of these three pillars.

With the Han board MSS in a private collection, these obstacles are exacerbated. Nothing is known about how the Han board MSS were acquired, and very little is known about their current caretaker (beyond a connection to Beijing), making provenance tracing futile for most scholars besides those, like Liu Huan, who are personally familiar with the collector. Access to the object, again, is severely restricted; this too makes arranging scientific testing difficult, if not impossible. Unlike a public institution, an anonymous collector is not

---

[50] "The art historian has traditionally had three major tools for determining the authenticity of a work of art, which can be listed in the order of their seeming capacity for 'truth': scientific analysis, historical documentation, and visual inspection by a knowing eye – or connoisseur." Francis V. O'Connor, "Authenticating the Attribution of Art: Connoisseurship and the Law in the Judging of Forgeries, Copies, and False Attributions," in Ronald D. Spencer, ed., *The Expert versus the Object: Judging Fakes and False Attributions in the Visual Arts* (Oxford: Oxford University Press, 2004), pp. 3–27 (at 6).

[51] Foster, "Introduction," 193.

beholden to any standards of academic ethics and can both control and/or manipulate the data made available to scholars when pursuing authentication.

Previously I have urged, as a generalized methodology, the identification of unanticipated, novel features on unprovenanced objects whose later confirmation on scientifically excavated artifacts can help establish a positive authentication.[52] This approach, however, does not accommodate negative appraisals (that is, identifying an object as a forgery), and in seeking "novelty" must prove an absence, which is a tenuous claim. Furthermore, authentication is inevitably a matter of "degrees of confidence" without absolute certainty. It is left to each researcher's discretion to determine what threshold evidence must pass to establish confidence and legitimate the object as a proper subject of responsible scholarship.[53] This is, of course, what Chinese scholars and Sinologists have done for centuries now, considering, for example, the uncertain textual histories behind many works in the received corpus.[54] As Valmisa argues in her section of this Element, many texts, newly unearthed and transmitted alike, are but "a well-informed reorganization of available materials within reasonable possibilities" by modern scholars (or, I would add, historical actors in various stages of a text's life), making them, in a sense, of "*our creation*" (emphasis by Valmisa).

Can minimum standards be established for this judgment? Is it enough to rely on the connoisseurship of experts? What if those experts are employed by the institutions that acquired the unprovenanced objects, or, in the case of the Han board MSS, hint at having a friendly relationship with the anonymous party or their colleagues – conflicts of interest, an issue Valmisa also has raised? Is it reasonable to expect *every* scholar to pursue their own detailed authentication of the unprovenanced artifacts they research, with the immense cost of time and energy this would entail? If not, then as Valmisa argues and as supported by Chao, transparency is imperative, which includes matters related to acquisition and access to materials, which are absent in the case of the Han board MSS and vague still for most institutional collections. Preliminary comments about the authenticity of the Han board MSS, primarily the *Cang Jie pian*, have been made by Zhang Chuanguan 張傳官 and other scholars.[55] No scientific analysis,

---

[52] Foster, "Introduction," 215–216.

[53] Foster, "Further Considerations," 464.

[54] Paul Fischer, "Authentication Studies (辨文學) Methodology and the Polymorphous Text Paradigm," *Early China* 32 (2008–9), 1–43. For an excellent survey and deconstruction of the concept of "authenticity" for the *shu* 書 corpus (e.g., the *Shangshu* 尚書), see Corina Smith, "'Authentic' *Venerated Documents*: What Are *Shu*, and What Is at Stake?" in Anke Hein and Christopher J. Foster, eds., *Understanding Authenticity in Chinese Cultural Heritage* (London: Routledge, 2023), pp. 221–234.

[55] Zhang Chuanguan 張傳官, "Tantan xinjian mudu *Cang Jie pian* de xueshu jiazhi 談談新見木牘蒼頡篇的學術價值," *Chutu wenxian yu guwenzi yanjiu* 出土文獻與古文字研究 9 (2020), 333–334, 350–351, with an initial draft published online at Fudan daxue chutu wenxian yu guwenzi

such as radiocarbon dating, has been conducted, however, and new archaeologically excavated parallels are still awaited.[56]

A more troubling question is how far to accept a mandate to salvage threatened cultural heritage already circulating illicitly. Indeed, taken further, this mandate could serve as justification for direct scholarly participation in the antiquities trade, purchasing unprovenanced objects and looted artifacts for study and donation to public institutions. Consider, for instance, the purchase and donation of Old Summer Palace bronze zodiac heads by Stanley Ho (in 2003 and 2007), or Cai Mingchao's disruptive bid (in 2009), which were praised as patriotic acts of repatriation and protest in Chinese media.[57] A similar logic previously bolstered European imperialist extraction of antiquities from China, Africa, and other regions, arguing that this was, in effect, salvaging the remnants of past civilizations important to world heritage from the uncertain stewardship of modern uncivilized caretakers.[58] If the market catalyst critique, when taken to the extreme, calls for forgoing the handling or study of any antiquities, the salvage principle, when similarly exaggerated, points to an unfettered market.

An unfettered market is clearly problematic, but I feel greater consideration is merited for finding ways to allow nonarchaeological interest groups to access cultural heritage while preserving archaeological context. Much of the discussion on the professional ethics of working with unprovenanced objects and looted artifacts has focused on mollifying *demand* for illicit antiquities while concurrently controlling the *supply* through strict legal enforcement.[59] On problems surrounding mollifying demand, in my prior article, I noted the enduring history of looting and complex motivations behind this, including, for instance, even the material value of items, like bronze vessels, made from precious metals.[60] I also questioned the sway my research may have on market

---

yanjiu zhongxin xuezhe wenku 復旦大學出土文獻與古文字研究中心學者文庫, December 25, 2019: www.gwz.fudan.edu.cn/Web/Show/4510; Foster, "Further Considerations," 459–460.

[56] Part of the problem is ascertaining the earliest reliable testimony for the Han board MSS. Liu Huan claims to have seen data in autumn 2009, and I have tried to corroborate Liu's account through internal evidence in the *Xinjian Han du* volume (Foster, "Further Considerations," 461–462), but the most conservative approach for now is to take publication of *Xinjian Han du* as the first appearance of the Han board MSS data.

[57] Both cases are discussed in Fiskesjö, "The Politics," 227–230; Murowchick, "'Despoiled,'" 28–29.

[58] "The key operative assumption was that the various non-Western civilizations were no longer viable ... other civilizations were generally seen as hopelessly 'past,' and whatever ruins and artifacts remained of them now had become the legitimate object of rescue operations, mounted by an enlightened vanguard of humanity: the West." Fiskesjö, "The Politics," 226.

[59] Yet, as Colin Renfrew asserts, "the underlying problem so far as antiquities are concerned is that the supply of legitimate antiquities is minimal." Renfrew, *Loot, Legitimacy, and Ownership*, 36.

[60] Foster, "Introduction," 236.

dynamics, namely the degree to which legitimation of these objects raises their value and generates demand. Here let me clarify: my point is not that colleagues in China ignore English scholarship.[61] Rather it is that the influence English scholarship has over public opinion in China and, specifically, on those actors directly involved in the looting trade (from the locals who help first dig up the artifacts, to the criminal networks that transport them, to the dealers and finally the end collectors) is less significant than the value it generates for advancing human knowledge and the restoration of potentially lost intellectual value. The glorification of tomb robbery conveyed by the novel series *Daomu biji* 盜墓筆記 and its TV and movie adaptations has a far greater audience and wider influence on the market, I suspect, than my niche English-language academic articles ever will.[62] This, of course, does not absolve scholars from a responsibility to voice contempt for looting and highlight the immense value of archaeological context in research; doing so can still minimize whatever negative effects scholarship has on the market.[63] But instead of eliminating academic study of the unprovenanced objects, a focus on public outreach efforts may prove more effective.[64]

[61] Compare to Friedrich, "Producing and Identifying," 330. On the engagement of Chinese scholars with Western Sinology, see Zhang Zhongwei's 張忠煒 review of Edward L. Shaughnessy's 2018 Chinese-language book, *Xiguan Han ji* 西觀漢記 (translated into English in 2019 as *Chinese Annals in the Western Observatory*). Zhang also comments on the debate over the ethics of working on unprovenanced bamboo strips: "Chutu wenxian yanjiu de haiwai jingjian – ping *Xiguan Han ji: Xifang Hanxue chutu wenxian yanjiu gaiyao* 出土文獻研究的海外鏡鑒——評《西觀漢記:西方漢學出土文獻研究概要》," *Guangmin ribao* 光民日報, August 21, 2019, plate 16, online: https://epaper.gmw.cn/gmrb/html/2019-08/21/nw.D110000gmrb_20190821_1-16.htm. I thank Paul Goldin for forwarding me this review when it first came out.

[62] Consider that the 2016 movie adaptation of *Daomu biji* (with the same Chinese title, translated into English as *Time Raiders*) was one of the most popular films in China when released, having now grossed more than $145,000,000, according to IMDB. Compare this to the 1,373 HTML views and 624 PDF views of my 2017 article, according to the metrics on the Society for the Study of Early China website (January 3, 2022). Nor does this simple comparison take into account the demographics of each audience; the latter I assume consists mostly of academics who are more likely to act as responsible custodians of cultural heritage.

[63] I emphasize this responsibility in light of Wylie's comment about "indirect harms" on claims that academic research has minimal market impact: "This is a contentious claim, but even if it were accepted … it seems most immediately aimed at critics who object that the publication of looted data causes direct harm, enhancing the value of antiquities and stimulating the market for them. It does not so clearly address … indirect harms: that such publication may 'tacitly legitimate' looting … reinforcing complacency about lootings and perhaps compromising the credibility [*sic*] archaeologists have when they take a public stand against the 'commercialization' of archaeological resources." Wylie, "Ethical Dilemmas," 169.

[64] Compare to Goldin, "The Problem," 149. Alder and Polk, "Stopping," 47: "This suggests that caution should be exercised in the simple assumption that criminal sanctions will 'fix' the problem. Attention needs to be paid explicitly to the matter of moral persuasion aimed at convincing potential consumers of the damage to their heritage that results from their purchase of unprovenanced antiquities." Alder and Polk then recommend the work of

Like any market, however, the trade in illicit antiquities is a function of not just demand, but also supply. This trade is comparable to (and indeed often concurrent with) that of other illicit goods, such as that of drugs or, as Valmisa discusses in her section of this Element, the trafficking of exotic animals and animal products.[65] On controlling supply through strict laws, Christine Alder and Kenneth Polk have noted that "one lesson that is available from criminological analysis of international illicit markets is that where demand remains at high levels in economically rich nations, it is naïve to assume that much can be gained by prohibitive legislation in source countries."[66] Pushing a market underground, moreover, brings a plethora of further issues, from making the traded objects harder to track (with a loss in public education and cultural exchange as artifacts are whisked away into private collections), to encouraging the creation of organized criminal networks and increased political corruption.[67] To relieve this dynamic, work needs to be done on minimizing demand for illicit antiquities (as championed by the market catalyst critique), and a role remains for criminal and civil law, both as symbolic ethical statements and as actual forms of deterrence.[68] At the same time, constructive avenues should also be pursued to open supply in ways that preserve archaeological context, even if just in the short term, to allow for a lasting redirection of demand.[69]

John Braithwaite on mitigating white collar crime. See also Colin Renfrew's praise for the work of Walter Alva in educating the local population at Sipan, Peru, and fostering a tourist industry around a site museum there, helping stifle once-rampant looting (*Loot, Legitimacy, and Ownership*, 62).

[65] Alder and Polk, "Stopping," 35–53. Alder and Polk do outline a few major differences too, including how (1) sales tend to be legal in market states; (2) antiquities are sold at exceptionally high prices; (3) clientele tend to be among the economic and social elite; and (4) the significance of transition ports to the trade (38–39).

[66] Ibid., 41.

[67] Ibid., 44. Alder and Polk anecdotally note that this is precisely what has happened with the trade in small Chinese jades: "There is impressionistic evidence that to some degree this has happened already with the trade in small jade objects that originate in China. These objects, because of their size and value, are relatively easy to move across national boundaries. There is, further, an enthusiastic and wealthy, if quite small, set of potential consumers who are quite willing to keep the trade out of general public and regulatory view. Once pushed underground, it will not be an easy task to bring it back into the wider public and regulatory view" (46).

[68] Ibid., 44–46.

[69] Murphy, *Plunder*, 143–180 and 157: "Once international demand is satisfied by the creation of a sizeable licit market, the profit is cut out of illicit trafficking and the concomitant anti-social behaviour is reduced. In a perfect model, money would be channeled toward preservation and study rather than to bribes. Scientists would replace thieves." The qualifier "international" is unnecessary. See also Alder and Polk, "Stopping," 50–51, and O'Keefe, *Trade*, 66–69. O'Keefe cautions that we should not assume a market will not expand to absorb the increased flow of antiquities, but continues: "these considerations should not prevent further study of the proposal and how it might be implemented . . . what is necessary is a short term means of satisfying demand so as to allow for other measures to operate to

Can other interest groups, nonarchaeological in nature, obtain greater access to a shared resource – cultural heritage – that shifts the enduring demand of consumers away from an underground illicit trade to a licit market? Patrick O'Keefe raises three options: disposals from collections, the enhancement of procedures for dealing with chance finds, and the distribution of finds from new excavations.[70] For example, in England, metal detecting is a popular and established hobby that potentially threatens archaeological context. The Treasure Act and the additional Portable Antiquities Scheme (hosted by the British Museum) help accommodate this interest group, both through a code of practice and dictating that finds are reported and left in situ for archaeological excavation by trained officials, but also outlining fair compensation to be given to metal detectorists who report their discovery.[71] Similar guidance is lacking in PRC law, where no space has been made that could accommodate such a hobby and compensation is left at the discretion of local officials.[72] Another avenue is working with commercial enterprises, beyond the salvage archaeology of cultural resource management, where privately funded projects (inclusive of international interests)[73] apply for PRC government permits and include trained archaeologists on staff for the collection of scientific data, but then also have a negotiated claim to a part of the finds for circulation in the legal antiquities market.[74] This is, in a sense, pursuing an alternative "temporary harm"

---

lessen or redirect demand in the long term" (68), measures such as rendering the collection of illicit antiquities antisocial (63).

[70] O'Keefe further remarks: "These methods have been advocated by others over the years but they have never before been formally considered by an intergovernmental body as a way of reducing the flow of antiquities from illegitimate sources." Ibid., 69, note 144.

[71] For the Portable Antiquities Scheme, see https://finds.org.uk, specifically, *Code of Practice for Responsible Metal Detecting in England and Wales* 2017 (https://finds.org.uk/getinvolved/ guides/codeofpractice). Renfrew, *Loot, Legitimacy, and Ownership*, 83–85, discusses metal detecting in England and Wales with an optimistic note about the valuable information he has obtained and the support the UK government has given the scheme.

[72] The feasibility of any such program may be questioned in China, where ancient sites are both prolific and often easily located, but this should not deter the discussion of policy options more appropriately tailored to the local circumstances.

[73] See Chao's section on interest groups, in particular her note of the tacit concessions PRC law makes to domestic antiquities markets. Chao also describes how working with commercial enterprises may also help relieve the budgetary and political tensions felt by local archaeological teams.

[74] "The old practice of *partage* of an archaeological excavation, between the overseas institutions in part funding the project on the one hand and the host country on the other, also has much to recommend it." Renfrew, *Loot, Legitimacy, and Ownership*, 21. See also the case of the *Hoi An* hoard, discussed by Alder and Polk ("Stopping," 52). This is problematized in Wylie, "Ethical Dilemmas," with the discussion of the Whydah controversy (175–180); it also risks many of the issues Chao describes with the early international partnerships between Western imperialist entities and China (she highlights in note 93 the relationship between Li Ji 李濟 and Carl Whiting Bishop), including who has "custodianship of excavated artifacts, whether they could be removed, who owned them, and thus who had

to achieve "long-term collective benefit," as discussed by Valmisa. Archaeological remains arguably are safest when left untouched in situ, as even scientific excavation is destructive and the methods employed today inevitably pale when compared to the technology of tomorrow. It is feasible, however, that the losses realized through managed and publicly documented excavation, which contributes in part to a licit market, may prove preferable to simply abandoning important data from looted artifacts already in circulation.

To Research or Boycott the Han Board Manuscripts?

In handling unprovenanced objects or looted artifacts, a scholar must "weigh between, on the one hand, the material and intellectual losses that may be suffered in the future by further incentivizing looting and, on the other hand, the material and intellectual losses we will suffer imminently by neglecting looted artifacts already on the market, as well as the future loss of neglecting those that may surface later."[75] This position is comparable to the conditional salvage principle, as Alison Wylie formulated (and critiqued) in her discussion of archaeological ethics: "Archaeologists should do what they can to salvage information from looted data *insofar as* it promises to be of scientific value, despite the loss of context and associations, and *insofar as* these interventions do not exacerbate the threat to archaeological resources posed by commercial exploitation (directly or indirectly)."[76] As opposed to the absolute in Wylie's second condition on exacerbating commercial exploitation, a relative valuation is necessary since even the study of legitimately and scientifically excavated artifacts can impact the market. It will always be a judgment call over precisely how much of a negative influence one is willing to tolerate.[77]

In the case of the Han board MSS, for my own part, I believe there is sufficient cause for concern to abstain from their dedicated study. This decision hinges on the lack of proper authentication, however; not necessarily the fact

---

the rights to them." Clear answers to these questions would need to be defined in any collaboration agreement.

[75] Foster, "Introduction," 233. Compare Valmisa's critique of suffering a temporary loss to achieve a long-term collective benefit, which is precisely the dynamic being weighed.

[76] Wylie, "Ethical Dilemmas," 171–172, with emphasis in the original. Wylie here introduces Christopher Donnan's defense of studying looted Moche culture remains from Peru, offering a charitable articulation of the logic motivating it. See the letter by Christopher B. Donnan, "Archaeology and Looting: Preserving the Record," in *Science* (1991), 498–499 (at 498). Other reactions to Donnan's work are found on 498–499.

[77] Wylie cites a number of cases documenting a relationship between academic publishing and the commercial value of antiquities, and discusses two in particular (including Thai Ban Chiang ceramics); see Wylie, "Ethical Dilemmas," 173–174.

that they are in a private collection.[78] Being in a private collection introduces new variables to weigh. There is, from the perspective of the market catalyst critique, the added risk of an untrustworthy caretaker who is not transparently accountable to PRC law or international agreements and potentially stands to profit from resale on the illicit antiquities markets. Yet this appears matched by the added urgency, according to the salvage principle, of the objects' precarious circumstances. Scholarship on the Han board MSS becomes an even more necessary means of rescuing the intellectual contribution of cultural heritage that now survives but stands imminently on the brink of being lost forever.

Systematic data on looting and shifts in the illicit antiquities market for wood and bamboo-strip manuscripts, such as the Han board MSS, are lacking, and the extent that scholarship impacts market dynamics – conceding that it does indeed have *some* impact – is unknown.[79] At best, anecdotal evidence and comparison to case studies for the trade in cultural heritage from other regions of the world allow for speculation.[80] It is hoped future studies can address these issues, and Chao provides insights for how to move forward in this regard. Until then, however, I favor salvaging a known quantity (e.g., the cultural heritage represented by the unprovenanced objects, here the Han board MSS) over attempting to preemptively rescue an unknown quantity (e.g., future losses of cultural heritage).[81] The Han board MSS are extant, they represent cultural heritage in threat, and have important information to share that can advance knowledge about China's past. It is unknown what losses may be suffered in the future, owing to the incremental incentivization supplied by studying the Han board MSS and adding to a larger collective body of scholarship on looted manuscripts. Goldin warns against underestimating the impact of scholarship on looted manuscripts, rightfully cautioning that "*disregarding* hidden costs does not *reduce* them" and usually "defer[s] the reckoning to future generations."[82]

---

[78] Let me be clear, however, that I do not condone the private collection of illicit antiquities and strongly urge the surrender of the Han board MSS to the responsible custodianship of a public institution.

[79] On the lack of data, see He, "Illicit Excavation," 19; Murowchick, "'Despoiled,'" 14. On this ambiguity in a different cultural context, Wylie writes: "It may be the case that the gold foil masks and strikingly beautiful ceramic art of the Moche would find a lucrative contemporary market no matter what archaeologists publish, or refrain from published, about its cultural significance … at the same time, there is a wide range of material whose marketability and market value is directly dependent, in various ways, on archaeological assessments of its significance." See "Ethical Dilemmas," 174.

[80] See the anecdotal evidence given in Foster, "Introduction," 238. Court cases trying looters of the Guodian cemetery may contradict my suggestion that bamboo strips were overlooked here previously. See the "Preliminary Verdict on the Case of Li Yihai Looting an Ancient Cultural Site and Tomb 李宜海盜掘古文化遺址古墓葬一審刑事判決書" and discussion in Maddalena Poli, "Preparing One's Act: Performance Supports and the Question of Human Nature in Early China," PhD dissertation, University of Pennsylvania (2022), pp. 24–34.

[81] Foster, "Introduction," 239.

[82] Goldin, "The Problem," 149.

Yet overestimating the impact of scholarship on looted manuscripts is also harmful, and *necessarily so*, both in the present and to future generations, by suppressing the production of knowledge and essentially forfeiting extant cultural heritage.

This judgment, however, is premised on the authenticity of the Han board MSS as Han-period artifacts that testify to ancient scribal practices. Without proper authentication, and with the salvage principle in mind, the nature of the Han board MSS as cultural heritage is uncertain. They might be looted ancient artifacts that bear invaluable data for the study of early China; they could equally be modern forgeries, which while significant perhaps for study of contemporary imaginations of China's past, would confuse and mislead scholarship on early China. Although initial analyses by scholars such as Zhang Chuanguan hint at a positive authentication as Han-period manuscripts, the threshold, in my opinion, has not yet been met to confidently treat them as genuinely ancient artifacts. That threshold likely will not be met until and if further scientifically excavated data appears in the future that can corroborate the Han board MSS data. Likewise, no sustained argument has yet been raised proving the Han board MSS to be modern forgeries. In light of this uncertainty, I will only make reference to the Han board MSS with extreme caution and with note of their compromised status.

The prior discussion has raised more questions than answers. Even should future studies provide more systematic data about the relationship between research on unprovenanced objects or looted artifacts and the incentivization of the illicit antiquities trade, many of the dilemmas encountered demand both treating the specifics of each case individually and ultimately applying rather subjective decision-making based on one's beliefs and value systems. This ranges from the sorts of authorities deemed just, to the risks taken when educating about the value of the past, to how far one is compelled to go to act upon their commitments. Appreciating this subjectivity, here I can only advocate, following Wylie in her discussion of the Society for American Archaeology's ethics policies (especially Principle No. 1), that researchers embrace a sense of "stewardship" to guide their contemplations on what limitations should be placed over scholarship on unprovenanced objects and looted artifacts.[83]

---

[83] Wylie, "Ethical Dilemmas," 183–187. Principle No. 1 "Stewardship":

> "The archaeological record, that is, in situ archaeological material and sites, archaeological collections, records and reports, is irreplaceable. It is the responsibility of all archaeologists to work for the long-term conservation and protection of the archaeological record by practicing and promoting stewardship of the archaeological record. Stewards are both caretakers of and advocates for the archaeological record for the benefit of all people; as they investigate and interpret the record, they should use the specialized knowledge they gain to promote public understanding and support for its long-term preservation." www.saa.org/career-practice/ethics-in-professional-archaeology.

Acknowledgments

I wish to thank Glenda Chao and Mercedes Valmisa for their collaboration, and the editors and anonymous reviewers for their guidance. Many other colleagues commented on earlier drafts, and I am very grateful for their insights and corrections. This section of this Element was composed during a British Academy Postdoctoral Fellowship at SOAS University of London. As a disclaimer, the statements expressed herein are given in a personal capacity only. This work is not affiliated with my current position at the Library of Congress, nor does it reflect views endorsed by the Library.

2 Where Does Responsibility Lie? Historical Contexts and the Ethics of the Cultural Custodianship of Source Materials (Glenda Ellen Chao)

Introduction

The destruction of cultural heritage is endemic to much of the world, and debate over how scholars ought to approach the use of unethically procured source materials is ongoing. China is certainly not unique in the world by any means when it comes to being a victim of looting because its long civilizational history has made it a very rich source of art and material culture for collectors, museums, and enthusiasts worldwide.[84] Likewise, the Chinese state is not unique in facing seemingly insurmountable challenges when it comes to protecting its cultural heritage.[85] My contribution to this conversation will address the question of whether to use unprovenienced sources in research from two related perspectives. The first is historical and focuses on how ethical decisions about using unprovenienced materials for research on early China is determined by the history of antiquarianism and the development of archaeology as a discipline in China.[86] The second perspective is about the consequences of this history for how we make ethical decisions in our research, which necessarily involves discussing who the proper custodians of cultural heritage in China are and where their responsibilities lie. I argue that different stakeholders within the realm of Chinese archaeology, including the Chinese government, Chinese archaeologists, international scholars, and regular consumers of antiquities both

---

[84] The coverage of illicit excavating and trade in antiquities is vast, so I list here only a few recent full-length studies on the subject that discuss different regions worldwide where looting and the trade in illicit antiquities is an ongoing problem; see, for instance, Renfrew, *Loot, Legitimacy, and Ownership*; Brodie et al., eds., *Trade in Illicit Antiquities*; Neil Brodie and Kathryn Walker Tubb, eds., *Illicit Antiquities: The Theft of Culture and the Extinction of Archaeology* (London: Routledge, 2002); Neil Brodie et al., eds., *Archaeology, Cultural Heritage, and the Antiquities Trade* (Gainesville: University of Florida Press, 2006); Paula Kay Lazrus and Alex W. Barker, eds., *All the King's Horses: Essays on the Impact of Looting and the Illicit Antiquities Trade on Our Knowledge of the Past* (Washington, DC: SAA Press, 2012).

[85] For good overviews of the various policies China has put in place to protect its cultural heritage over the past century, and some of the challenges these policies have faced since their enactments, please see Murphy, *Plunder*; Michael L. Dutra, "Sir, How Much Is That Ming Vase in the Window? Protecting Cultural Relics in the People's Republic of China," *Asian-Pacific Law & Policy Journal* 5 (2004), 62–100; Murowchick, "'Despoiled'"; Guolong Lai, "The Emergence of 'Cultural Heritage' in Modern China: A Historical and Legal Perspective," in Akira Matsuda and Luisa Elena Mengoni, eds., *Reconsidering Cultural Heritage in East Asia* (London: Ubiquity Press, 2016), pp. 47–87.

[86] I take "unprovenienced" here to mean artifacts whose exact in situ archaeological context cannot be determined due to the conditions under which they were removed from the ground. This term can cover looted objects as well as those whose excavation histories are murky or unknown. It is different from the term "unprovenanced," which I use in this section of this Element to refer to the artifacts in private or public collections whose ownership histories are either murky or unknown.

within China and abroad, each bear a portion of the responsibility of protecting China's intangible cultural heritage. We have to consider wider structural and institutional factors related to how Chinese archaeology and early China studies have developed as fields of study in order to better determine best practices for each interest group. I close with a brief discussion about what steps can be taken in the future to begin to ameliorate the problem of looting from which these ethical questions arise. I ultimately propose that it is the valuation of cultural heritage across stakeholder groups that matters most in beginning to change the situation for the better.

A Historical Approach to an Ethical Question: Antiquarianism, Archaeology, and Nationalism in China

The big question this collaborative Element is trying to answer is relatively straightforward: is using unprovenienced materials in early China studies and Chinese archaeology ethical? The answer, however, is much more complex than simply yes or no because of the historical conditions under which the field of early China studies and Chinese archaeology have emerged, which we must first understand.

The Ethics of the Antiquarian Legacy

While large-scale destruction of cultural heritage is a phenomenon that enters public consciousness in waves in the modern era, smaller-scale destruction has a much longer and more constant history. One such practice is known as antiquarianism, here defined as the "systematic preoccupation with the material remains of the past . . . motivated by an interest in the past as such."[87] During the Northern Song Dynasty (CE 960–1127), this practice gave birth to *jinshixue* 金石学 ("study of metal and stone"), which spurred the collecting and preservation of antiquities among educated elites. One of the legacies of the *jinshixue* tradition, which lasted all the way into the modern period, are records of scholarship on artifacts collected into catalogs; the most famous of these are

---

[87] See Lothar von Falkenhausen, "Antiquarianism in East Asia: A Preliminary Overview," in Alain Schnapp, ed., *World Antiquarianism: Comparative Perspectives (Issues & Debates)* (Los Angeles, CA: Getty Research Institute Press, 2014), pp. 35–67. In actuality, antiquarianism is middle-period branch of a much broader and more nebulous practice of *fugu* 復古 ("returning to the ancient"), which emerges as early as the second millennium BCE in deliberate archaism within early bronze art; for more on this, see Wu Hung, "Introduction," in Wu Hung, ed., *Reinventing the Past: Archaism and Antiquarianism in Chinese Art and Visual Culture* (Chicago, IL: University of Chicago Press, 2010), pp. 9–46. For more information on antiquarianism in general, see Alain Schnapp, ed., *World Antiquarianism: Comparative Perspectives* (Los Angeles, CA: Getty Research Institute Press, 2013). For comparative studies on antiquarianism across Eurasia, see Peter N. Miller and François Louis, eds., *Antiquarianism and Intellectual Life in Europe and China, 1500–1800* (Ann Arbor: University of Michigan Press, 2012).

the *kaogutu* 考古圖 and the *bogutu* 博古圖, though others, especially from the Qing period (CE 1644–1911), also exist.[88]

These catalogs, which usually contain descriptions of objects, rubbings, transcriptions and translations of inscriptions, sometimes drawings, and so forth, are potentially useful sources of information for scholars today. However, because many of the artifacts contained in these catalogs are either unprovenienced or have very murky proveniences, they are nevertheless both ethically and methodologically questionable as source materials for scholarship. If we use these materials in our research, are we potentially violating the ethical code not to support the destruction of cultural heritage? To this, I would say probably not, as many of the artifacts described in the catalogs were removed, lost, or even destroyed long before modern scholars were even in a position to make ethical choices. Foster also rightly points out that scholarship on early China has long incorporated unprovenienced artifacts, particularly oracle bones and bronze vessels, and that even if an artifact is unprovenienced, it does not necessarily mean that it was looted.

Methodologically, however, I would caution against over-relying on these catalogs to make inferences about the distant past. To echo Valmisa, antiquarian sources are not only incomplete evidence, but they are making knowledge claims on their own. In other words, they are secondary sources of evidence on early China, not primary ones, and as such, they are better gauges for how past scholars *thought* about the study of early China rather than sources for accurate information on early China itself. The antiquarian legacy demonstrates that in many cases, methodological concerns can and ought to overlap with ethical ones.

Ethics and the Legacies of Imperialism and the Birth of Scientific Archaeology in China

Modern archaeology in China has roots in the antiquarian tradition as *jinshixue* continued as an elite pastime well into the nineteenth and twentieth centuries.[89]

---

[88] For excellent studies on late imperial Chinese antiquarianism and the role these two catalogs have played in preserving and transmitting the antiquarian tradition, see Shana J. Brown, *Pastimes: From Art and Antiquarianism to Modern Chinese Historiography* (Honolulu: University of Hawaii Press, 2011); Jeffrey Moser, "The Ethics of Immutable Things: Interpreting Lü Dalin's Illustrated Investigations of Antiquity," *Harvard Journal of Asiatic Studies* 72.2 (2012), 259–293; Jeffrey Moser, "Why Cauldrons Come First: Taxonomic Transparency in the Earliest Chinese Antiquarian Catalogues," *Journal of Art Historiography*, no. 11 (2014), 1–23; Yunchiahn C. Sena, *Bronze and Stone: The Cult of Antiquity in Song Dynasty China* (Seattle: University of Washington Press, 2019).

[89] Falkenhausen has rightly pointed out as well that one of the lasting legacies of the antiquarian tradition on Chinese archaeology even today is the latter's focus on using archaeological material to verify and expand text-based constructions of history that very much serve broader nationalistic

During the late Qing period, concepts of heritage preservation were introduced from Western imperialists and were adopted by the Chinese state in its efforts to modernize and to retain centralized control over the country. In this process, antiquarian traditions of preserving, protecting, and studying objects from the past were folded into state-sponsored policies aimed at preserving "national heritage," which itself was a new concept that emerged as a rhetorical and symbolic tool to mobilize the Chinese populace in the transformation of China into a modern nation-state.[90] Scientific archaeology, with its emphasis on empiricism and fieldwork, was introduced within this same context of national self-rediscovery and self-strengthening in the face of Western imperialism, and was spurred on by the desire of many intellectuals to use the idea of *fugu* 復古 ("returning to the ancient") not to venerate the past, but to help process and appraise the social, political, and cultural fluctuations they were experiencing as well as to find a fresh path to national progress.[91]

Ironically, the earliest archaeological projects undertaken during this era were collaborations between European archaeologists and Chinese archaeologists who were trained in the West, such as the excavation of Yangshao 仰韶 village in 1921 led by geologists Johan Gunnar Andersson (1874–1960) from Sweden and Yuan Fuli 袁福禮 (1893–1987) from Henan. In this case and in many others, European, American, and even Japanese institutions involved themselves by providing funding to take part in the work, which had the side benefit of allowing these institutions direct access to excavated artifacts. In the late nineteenth and early twentieth centuries, imperialists like Aurel Stein benefited from the relative weakness of the Qing state to remove large quantities of cultural relics from sites he "discovered" at Dunhuang 敦煌 in Gansu 甘肅 province. By the late 1920s, however, the reach of imperial greed was beginning to be checked by Chinese archaeologists as described earlier in this Element, leaving imperial powers only partnerships as an avenue to attempt to acquire the

---

and patriotic ends; see Falkenhausen, "Antiquarianism," 35–67. Another major lasting legacy of the antiquarian tradition on modern Chinese archaeology is the use of nomenclatures first established by *jinshixue* scholars as the foundation for typology and classification; for more on this history as well as modern challenges to this tradition, see Lothar von Falkenhausen, "On the Historiographical Orientation of Chinese Archaeology," *Antiquity* 67 (1993), 839–849; see also Anke Hein, "The Problem of Typology in Chinese Archaeology," *Early China* 39 (2016), 21–52.

[90] For more on this, see Lai, "The Emergence of 'Cultural Heritage' in Modern China," 47–87. Magnus Fiskesjö has also written on this topic; see Magnus Fiskesjö, "The Politics," 225–245; see also Magnus Fiskesjö, *China before China: Johan Gunnar Andersson, Ding Wenjiang, and the Discovery of China's Prehistory* (Stockholm: Museum of Far Eastern Antiquities, 2004) and Magnus Fiskesjö, "Rescuing the Empire: Chinese Nation-Building in the Twentieth Century," *European Journal of East Asian Studies* 5 (2006), 15–44.

[91] For more on this, see Guolong Lai, "Digging Up China: Imperialism, Nationalism, and Regionalism in the Yinxu Excavation, 1928–1937," in Bonnie Effros and Guolong Lai, eds., *Unmasking Ideology in Imperial and Colonial Archaeology* (Berkeley: University of California Press, 2018), pp. 87–88.

pieces for which the international art market was beginning to clamor.[92] While not all international partnerships were poorly intentioned, some high-profile early ones were, and falling-outs usually concerned the custodianship of excavated artifacts, whether they could be removed, who owned them, and thus who had the rights to them.[93] These examples illustrate the complicated entanglements between nationalism, Western imperialism, and the appreciation and collecting of cultural relics both domestic and international that influenced the development of antiquarianism into scientific archaeology and cultural heritage protection in China in the early to mid-twentieth century.

Moving forward, I do not believe that scholars can continue to comfortably ignore this connection. We might not have the power to recover original in situ contexts, and thus it might be just as well that we continue to use these collections because otherwise they would have been looted for nothing (academically speaking), but we should at least acknowledge the problematic histories of these collections when we use them. To be clear, I am not advocating that we disregard all work that has been done with the help of previously looted artifacts. I am simply suggesting that there are ways we can incorporate recognition of our privilege within ongoing work. One good example is Adam Smith's study on the Ernest K. Smith collection of Shang 商 divination inscriptions at Columbia University where he devotes a section to the history of the collection, pointing out especially its dubious connection with a supposedly stolen box of bones and shells from the Yinxu 殷墟 excavations that were halted in 1929.[94]

Ethics and Chinese Archaeology since the Mid-twentieth Century

Since 1949, several major developments in Chinese archaeology have made lasting impacts on the conditions under which scholars today can make ethical decisions regarding unprovenienced artifacts. The first was the doubling down on the part of the government of the newly established PRC under the Chinese Communist Party (CCP) on the use of archaeology to serve nation-building ends, specifically in validating Marxist ideology and historiography. To this end, the period from 1949 to roughly 1979 was marked by preoccupation on the

---

[92] See Justin M. Jacobs, *The Compensations of Plunder: How China Lost Its Treasures* (Chicago, IL: University of Chicago Press, 2020) for an excellent historical study of how this process occurred.

[93] One such situation arose between Li Ji 李濟 and Carl Whiting Bishop. For more on this relationship and how it represents tensions between intellectuals on both sides of the Western imperialism divide, see Lai, "Digging Up China," 92–97.

[94] Adam Smith, "The Ernest K. Smith Collection of Shang Divination Inscriptions at Columbia University and the Evidence for Scribal Training at Anyang," in Matthew Rutz and Morag M. Kersel, eds., *Archaeologies of Text: Archaeology, Technology, Ethics* (Oxford: Oxbow Books, 2014), pp. 121–141.

part of historians and archaeologists in finding evidence of the unilineal social evolutionary stages espoused by Marxist thinkers like Lewis Henry Morgan (1877) and Friedrich Engels (1884) and identifying them with known periods of Chinese history.[95] At the same time, aggressive economic and social projects undertaken by the new regime resulted in both the discovery and the destruction of a great quantity of archaeological sites and cultural relics.[96]

Since the 1980s and the reopening of China to the West, there has not only been a surge of interest in scientific techniques in archaeology such as radiocarbon dating, but also an increasing movement away from Marxist modes of scholarship toward deeper recognition of the regional variety. This same period saw the discovery and excavation of a huge number of major archaeological sites. This golden age of archaeological work was helped along by the adoption of scientific techniques such as radiocarbon dating; by the establishment of national publishing houses (e.g., Wenwu Publishing House 文物出版社) dedicated to the printing and distribution of archaeological periodicals, site reports, and related content; and a newfound commitment on the part of the CCP to establishing a systemized bureaucracy under which all archaeological and heritage preservation work was to be done.[97] This institutional framework survives today, though one of its major drawbacks that has implications for our ethics question, which I will discuss in more detail, has to do with the tensions between various levels of the archaeological bureaucracy regarding funding, prestige, and access to sites.[98]

The final major development in Chinese archaeology since 1949 has to do with cultural heritage management. After 1949, the CCP clamped down on the looting and destruction of cultural heritage that was rampant during the 1930s and earlier. Part of the impetus behind this was nationalistic, of course. According to Tong Enzheng, it was important to the CCP that antiquities be retained domestically because their protection was regarded as a legitimation of the regime as well as a rebuke about the looting and destruction Western imperialists caused during the last decades of the Qing Dynasty.[99] One of the ways the CCP achieved this was to severely limit the degree to which foreigners

---

[95] Tong Enzheng, "Thirty Years of Chinese Archaeology," in Philip L. Kohl and Clare Fawcett, eds., *Nationalism, Politics, and the Practice of Archaeology* (Cambridge: Cambridge University Press, 1995), pp. 177–197 (at 180–182).

[96] For a list of some of the major discoveries that took place in China from 1949 to 1977, see K. C. Chang, "Chinese Archaeology since 1949," *Journal of Asian Studies* 36.4 (1977), 623–646 (at 626–634).

[97] Ibid. See also Murphy, *Plunder*, 77–142; Dutra, "Sir, How Much Is That Ming Vase in the Window?"; Murowchick, "'Despoiled'"; Lai, "The Emergence of 'Cultural Heritage' in Modern China."

[98] For more detail on these tensions, see Erika E. S. Evasdottir, *Obedient Autonomy: Chinese Intellectuals and the Achievement of Orderly Life* (Honolulu: University of Hawaii Press, 2004), pp. 112–115.

[99] Tong, "Thirty Years of Chinese Archaeology," 183.

could participate in archaeological work in China or even learn about what was going on.[100] While this situation was ameliorated after the 1980s, it remains a requirement that foreign archaeologists obtain a partnership with a Chinese domestic institution in order to conduct archaeological fieldwork.[101]

This era also saw the promulgation of the first laws regarding the treatment of archaeological materials and cultural heritage. Currently, China's Law on the Protection of Cultural Relics (LPCR), updated most recently in 2002, contains stipulations regarding several important aspects of cultural heritage management, including, among others, the ownership of all underground cultural relics as well as those located in inland territorial waters, proper procedures for conducting archaeological fieldwork, movement of cultural relics across national borders as well as among state and private collections, and the responsibilities delegated to local administrative bodies on the protection of cultural heritage.[102]

The impact of these developments on Chinese archaeology are manifold, not least because they reinforce the connection between archaeology, politics, and nationalism that has existed for the Chinese state since the early 1900s. Moreover, the history of cultural heritage protection and archaeology in China has led to a complicated set of ethical conditions for scholars to operate under today, and in the second half of my section of this Element, I will begin to unpack some of what this complicated history means for us.

Ethical Operators: Who Are the Custodians of Cultural Heritage and What Are Our Responsibilities?

One of the major takeaways of the history just outlined for scholars today is the realization that we are inextricably bound up in the web of structures that make up the current system in which cultural heritage is being unethically exploited. This does not mean that it is our fault, or that the responsibility for changing the system lies solely with us. In Foster's words, the key issue is who controls

---

[100] According to Tong, foreign scholars were only allowed access to data formally published in the three national journals, *Kaogu* 考古, *Wenwu* 文物, and *Kaogu Xuebao* 考古学报; see ibid., 189; see also, Jacobs, *The Compensations of Plunder*, 228–270.

[101] See, for instance, the Measures for the Administration of Foreign-Related Archaeological Activities, which was promulgated in 1991. For more on this measure, see Murowchick, "'Despoiled,'" 20.

[102] People's Republic of China, State Council, Law of the People's Republic of China on the Protection of Cultural Relics, adopted November 19, 1982, article 5, https://english.www.gov .cn/archive/laws_regulations/2014/08/23/content_281474982987444.htm. See also Murphy, *Plunder*, 77–149; Dutra, "Sir, How Much Is That Ming Vase in the Window?"; Murowchick, "'Despoiled'"; Fiskesjö, "The Politics," 225–245; Zhuang Min, "The Administration of China's Archaeological Heritage," in Henry Cleere, ed., *Archaeological Heritage Management in the Modern World* (London: Routledge, 1989), pp. 102–108.

access to cultural heritage and who decides and sanctifies best practices. As I argue in what follows, several main interest groups bear different portions of the responsibility of acting as custodians and gatekeepers of China's cultural heritage; these include the Chinese government, Chinese archaeologists, and international scholars. Consumers of antiquities and regular Chinese citizens need to be mentioned as well. I say that each group bears a *portion* of the full responsibility because while there are overlaps in the roles that each group has regarding their ideal mandate, custody of cultural heritage is the responsibility of an entire system and a network of groups of individuals rather than any single group alone.

Interest Groups: The State, Chinese Archaeologists, and the International Scholarly Community

The Chinese government (aka the state) bears a large responsibility for safeguarding cultural heritage by setting the terms of how Chinese antiquities are valued and perceived in the modern world. Unfortunately, some current policies, such as the LPCR, introduce problematic ambiguities. For instance, Dutra has noted that the LPCR permits Chinese citizens, legal persons, and other organizations to collect cultural relics obtained through inheritance or gifting, through purchasing from relics shops and auction enterprises, and through exchange, transfer, or other authorized method.[103] Additional provisions, specifically articles 53 through 58, are made for the opening and running of cultural relics stores and auction enterprises, including regulations for how and when cultural relics should be examined and approved by the state when they enter this domestic market. Given that article 64 makes it illegal to excavate, destroy, smuggle, or in any way disturb or damage cultural relics without state authorization, it raises the question of where the cultural relics that are meant to circulate through these stores and auction houses are originating. Together, these provisions lead some scholars to believe that the LPCR not only recognizes the prevailing reality that China has a burgeoning domestic market for cultural relics,[104] but also facilitates its domestic growth.[105] Foster's discussion

---

[103] Dutra, "Sir, How Much Is That Ming Vase in the Window?" 83. See also People's Republic of China, State Council, Law of the People's Republic of China on the Protection of Cultural Relics, adopted November 19, 1982, article 50, https://english.www.gov.cn/archive/laws_regu lations/2014/08/23/content_281474982987444.htm.

[104] Dutra, "Sir, How Much Is That Ming Vase in the Window?" 84. Fiskesjö also notes that "officials charged with protecting cultural sites must contend with commercial and industrial interests, which may be favored by other branches of government. On top of this, the superficially monolithic notion of Chinese society has less and less validity, as 'heritage authorities' and archaeologists, in a struggle over values and their definition, face mounting opposition and disagreement from domestic antiquities dealers and auctioneers, who prefer to see an increased supply of goods for their rapidly expanding trade inside China." See Fiskesjö, "The Politics," 237.

[105] Murowchick, "'Despoiled,'" 27.

of the murky circumstances surrounding the acquisition of the Han board MSS speaks to these scholars' concerns.

In addition, article 3 proclaims the existence of a multitiered gradation system under which all cultural relics, which we can only assume includes all known and discoverable materials, are classified, including "valuable" and "ordinary" categories under which are grade one through grade three cultural relics. The article does not stipulate what specific types of cultural relics might be included under any category or grade, though we might be able to infer from article 1 of the current memorandum of understanding between the United States and China that important cultural relics include metal, ceramic, stone, textual, glass, and painting artifacts dating from the Paleolithic period until the end of the Tang Dynasty (ca. 75,000 BCE–907 CE) as well as monumental sculptures more than 250 years old.[106] Both Murowchick and Dutra note the dismaying vagueness of this article, saying not only that judgment on gradation is likely to be based on equally undefined "specialist appraisers," but also that the ambiguity of this provision means that only the most valuable or precious relics will be given priority in terms of protection, leaving the remainder to local administrations whose budgets might not provide for the best preservation and protection possible.[107] Lack of clarity from the top like this ensures that provincial and municipal archaeological workers and their counterparts based at universities have a hard time fulfilling their roles as conscientious scholars and educators as well.

Chinese archaeologists also bear a portion of the responsibility for safeguarding cultural heritage due to their proximity to the sites and relics themselves. Their specific mandates, however, are often contradictory and difficult to carry out. For instance, the LPCR stipulates in articles 8 and 9 not only that "local people's governments at various levels shall take charge of the work concerning the protection of cultural relics within their own administrative areas," but that they "attach importance to the protection of cultural relics and correctly handle the relations between economic and social development and the protection of cultural relics so as to ensure safety of the cultural relics."[108] In addition, article 10 claims that budgets for carrying out this work are dependent upon revenues generated by local bureaus through state-owned museums and tourist sites, donations, and the establishment of social funds

---

[106] Article 1 of the Memorandum of Understanding between the United States of America and China, signed at Beijing, January 10, 2019.

[107] Ibid., 22; see also Dutra, "Sir, How Much Is That Ming Vase in the Window?" 86.

[108] See People's Republic of China, State Council, Law of the People's Republic of China on the Protection of Cultural Relics, adopted November 19, 1982, articles 8 and 9, https://english .www.gov.cn/archive/laws_regulations/2014/08/23/content_281474982987444.htm.

for the protection of cultural relics.[109] Taken together, these policies create a situation in which local bureaus of cultural relics administration are often limited in their ability to protect the cultural relics within their jurisdictions, first because of low funding that can be increased only through the exploitation of cultural relics that need protecting,[110] and second because, according to article 9, they have to balance the needs of economic and social development within their administrative territories with scientific excavation. As a result of this mandate, excavation in China usually takes place not as long-term research-oriented projects, but more often as salvage or rescue projects, where archaeologists have only a few months to excavate what they can from a site before it is paved over by new construction.[111]

Arguably, international scholars are some of the least able to affect the way cultural heritage is safeguarded in China with neither the power to create public policy nor on-the-ground access to cultural heritage sites. What we do seem to have control over, however, is perception and interpretive influence. As Goldin argues, "looting is fueled by the extraordinary value of authenticated artifacts on the antiquities market, and consequently researchers who contribute to authenticating them are effectively complicit."[112] In other words, scholarship has the potential to contribute to looting because by authenticating looted antiquities during the process of using them as part of our scholarship, we are not only benefiting from the destruction, but also sending no signal of condemnation against it. Goldin's position is valid, though Foster rightly cautions that self-censorship among the scholarly community can also be a slippery slope toward being unable to identify where the boundaries of complicity are, from scholarship that focuses on looted sources to secondary or even tertiary scholarship that merely cites those sources. He also rightly points out that any boycotting of looted source material is only effective if it is universal (or at least very widespread), as the choice for only some scholars to refrain does nothing to address the original point that scholarship contributes to looting.

Valmisa approaches the question from a different angle, arguing that publishing on unprovenienced artifacts can have a positive impact if it is done in transparent ways, which could provide the scholarly community with the power to demand that the system change to a certain degree. To me, this means several things. First, we

---

[109] See People's Republic of China, State Council, Law of the People's Republic of China on the Protection of Cultural Relics, adopted November 19, 1982, article 10, https://english.www.gov .cn/archive/laws_regulations/2014/08/23/content_281474982987444.htm.

[110] For more detail on this system, see Evasdottir, *Obedient Autonomy*, pp. 98–136.

[111] For an excellent overview of the early history of salvage (aka "rescue") archaeology in China, see Di Yin Lu, "From Trash to Treasure: Salvage Archaeology in the People's Republic of China, 1951–1976," *Modern China* 42.4 (2016), 415–443.

[112] Goldin, "The Problem," 145. He has written similarly in the past; see Goldin, "Heng Xian," 152–160.

need to take a stance on the authenticity of the artifact or corpus with reference to group consensus. Second, we need to openly discuss any problematic associations the object or corpus might have with historical violence, deliberate iconoclasm, or imperialism. Third, we need to acknowledge when research has been done in conjunction with collectors. Finally, we need to recognize that any information gleaned from the study of a looted object is incomplete, and so we should make an effort to balance its use with as many other kinds of source materials as possible in order to craft a more holistic narrative of the past.

I also believe that it entails rethinking the methodologies with which we approach the study of early China in two ways. First, we need to encourage more multi- and interdisciplinary work that actively marries archaeological and textual research questions with their concomitant sources. This kind of work will help us avoid overreliance on any one kind of source material, flawed as they both usually are due to problems of provenience. Second, it might be fruitful for the field to reconsider the end goal of our research. Valmisa makes the very valid point that any knowledge claims we make based on unprovenienced texts are in essence *our creations*, and not truthful reconstructions of the past. I believe that if we relinquish reconstruction as a goal of our research and embrace the idea that we are creating *possibilities*, we also relinquish the feeling that if we do not study unprovenienced artifacts, then we are somehow not achieving the most complete representation of the past that we can. We can stop feeling as though our scholarship is deficient for not utilizing every source possible, looted or not. This speaks somewhat to Goldin's claim that the way we value antiquities matters to what drives looting and is a point I will return to in the conclusion.

Interest Groups: Consumers and Looters

The interest groups discussed earlier in this section are all directly involved in the production of archaeological knowledge, and thus together, they bear a large portion of the responsibility of acting as custodians and ethical arbiters of cultural heritage. But what about average consumers of cultural heritage like museum goers versus the museum institutions themselves, versus private collectors? In my view, average consumers of cultural heritage like museum goers bear the least responsibility because they are most likely unaware of the ethical problems involved. On the other hand, collectors – and this includes both private collectors and museums – bear a far greater portion of the responsibility because they directly contribute to the ongoing problem of looting by being *the* market that looting supplies. Certainly, international legislation like the 1970 UNESCO Convention[113] and concomitant

---

[113] The United Nations Education, Scientific and Cultural Organization, Convention on the Means of Prohibiting and Preventing Illicit Import, Export and Ownership of Cultural Property, adopted November 14, 1970, at the General Conference at its sixteenth session, Paris.

domestic legislation like, in the United States at least, the 1983 Cultural Property Implementation Act,[114] and the Cultural Property Advisory Committee,[115] are aimed at making it harder for both museums and individual private collectors to acquire looted antiquities, but international laws are most effective at stopping items from crossing borders; they are powerless to curb domestic consumption, which is a problem of increasing urgency in China especially.[116]

Foster also notes that in China at least, a trend has emerged of wealthy Chinese citizens purchasing previously looted cultural relics off the antiquities market and donating them back to the state to great domestic and international acclaim.[117]Additionally, article 12 of the LPCR claims that the state encourages donations of cultural relics from personal collections and that such actions will be rewarded through material means.[118] We can decry this political use of cultural relics as harmful because it encourages and glorifies art collecting, but we cannot deny the power that cultural relics have in inciting modern nation-states to pay attention to the past.

Can a balance be struck regarding the state's manipulation of art collecting and scholars' use of these materials in their research? This question bears further consideration.

Finally, what about the looters themselves? Chinese archaeologists at the municipal or county level usually know about a vast quantity of potential archaeological sites within their jurisdictions, often more than they can excavate in any given year, and certainly far more than they can actively guard.[119]

---

[114] The Senate and House of Representatives of the United States of America in Congress, Convention on Cultural Property Implementation Act, Public Law 100–204 [H.R. 1777], 101 Stat. 1331, approved December 22, 1987.

[115] This committee is comprised of eleven presidentially appointed members responsible for receiving and assessing requests for import restrictions submitted to the United States by foreign governments alongside considering proposals to exist existing agreements and actions, reviewing current import restrictions, and reporting findings to the Department of State.

[116] According to Murowchick, there were estimates of some 90 million antique collectors in China in the year 2010, which gives you at least a very small idea of scale of the problem of collecting; see Murowchick, "'Despoiled,'" 26.

[117] Magnus Fiskesjö has also written about this, stating that "such patriotic initiatives unfold in close concert with government agencies and policies, which over the last decade have already allowed dealers and auctioneers to rapidly develop a hugely profitable market for art and antiquities, gathered under the banner of 'patriotism'"; see Fiskesjö, "The Politics," 225.

[118] People's Republic of China, State Council, Law of the People's Republic of China on the Protection of Cultural Relics, adopted November 19, 1982, article 12/paragraph 3, https://english.www.gov.cn/archive/laws_regulations/2014/08/23/content_281474982987444.htm.

[119] There have been attempts to comprehensively document and publish all known archaeological and cultural relics sites in China over the years. See, for instance, Guojia Wenwuju bian 國家文物局編, eds., *Disanci quanguo wenwu pucha baida xinfaxian* 第三次全國文物普查百大新發現 ("100 New Discoveries of the Third Nationwide Survey of Cultural Heritage") (Beijing 北京: Wenwu chubanshe 文物出版社, 2011); Guojia Wenwuju bian 國家文物局編, eds., *2008 nian disanci quanguo wenwu pucha zhongyao xinfaxian* 2008年第三次全國文物普查重要新發現 ("Important Discoveries of the Third Nationwide Survey of Cultural Heritage, 2008")

However, this knowledge is made possible only by archaeologists' deep ties with the local communities from which they often come themselves, and from which they usually recruit extra workers for their digs. The local communities don't necessarily have the same vested interest in preserving archaeological sites for future excavation, and many end up being well-trained to detect and periodize pottery sherds through their ties with active excavations.[120] At the same time, Foster raises the important issue that some local communities might feel they have rights or ownership over unearthed remains, especially if they see themselves as either the lineal descendants of ancient communities, or, as Jada Ko argues, as indigenous to the archaeological experience of their localities.[121] Valmisa also points out that looters are part of the community that archaeological knowledge ostensibly intends to benefit. In these cases, scholars cannot blame local communities for attempting to use their cultural heritage how they see fit. Rather, it should be the responsibility of the state to ensure that proper incentives are in place to discourage looting for profit, something that the current LPCR and its enforcement apparatus does not seem well positioned to do. One avenue for change might be to take seriously Foster's suggestion of allowing nonarchaeological interest groups greater access to shared resources like cultural heritage enacted outside of China, or even more tantalizingly, involving local communities more deeply in decision-making surrounding the excavation, display, narration, and preservation of archaeological sites.[122]

(Beijing 北京: Wenwu chubanshe 文物出版社, 2009). These documentation efforts also come in the form of cartographic material; see, for instance, Guojia wenwuju zhubian 國家文物局主編, eds., *Zhongguo wenwu dituji* 中國文物地圖集 ("Map of Cultural Relics in China") (Xi'an 西安: Xi'an ditu chubanshe 西安地圖出版社, 1989). Following the publication of this volume, the Cultural Relics Bureau proceeded to publish volumes of these cultural relics maps for each province; see, for instance, Guojia wenwuju zhubian 國家文物局主編, eds., *Zhongguo wenwu dituji: Hubei fence* 中國文物地圖集:湖北分冊 ("Map of Cultural Relics in China: Volume on Hubei"), 2 vols. (Xi'an 西安: Xi'an ditu chubanshe 西安地圖出版社, 2002).

[120] For more detailed discussion of the complex negotiations in which archaeologists and local communities engage, see Evasdottir, *Obedient Autonomy*, pp. 173–210.

[121] Ko demonstrates through ethnographic study of the Dongxiang 東鄉Muslim residents around the Qijiaping 齊家平 site in Gansu 甘肅 province, that even though this community is not indigenous to the Qijiaping area, they nevertheless feel a connection to the landscape created through several decades of involvement with archaeological digs. This, she argues, is a narrative that, if properly emphasized, can benefit heritage preservation efforts throughout China. See Jada Ko, "Remembering Qijiaping, Forgetting Qijiaping: Archaeological Experience As Shared Heritage," *Bulletin of the Museum of Far Eastern Antiquities* 82 (2021), 135–180.

[122] This latter strategy was enacted at the site of the tombs of Sipan of the Moche culture on the north coast of Peru to great success. See Sidney D. Kirkpatrick, *Lords of Sipan: A Tale of Pre-Inca Tombs, Archaeology, and Crime* (New York: William Morrow and Company, 1992).

Conclusions: Where Do We Go from Here?

The most immediate answer to the question of whether we should use unprovenienced artifacts and texts in our scholarship is to say that in an ideal world, we could legislate the problem of looting away so that new sources only come to us through scholarly and scientific means; certainly many aspects of China's situation would benefit from more nuanced and careful policymaking. To think through what kinds of new legislation might be beneficial, we can draw upon work that has been done previously on analyzing and quantifying the current market for antiquities worldwide. Tess Davis, for example, has analyzed more than twenty years of information from Sotheby's Auction House's sales of Indian and Southeast Asian Art in New York to show that despite the 1970 UNESCO Convention, the vast majority of Khmer art auctioned by Sotheby's likely has an illicit origin.[123] Similarly, Elizabeth Gilgan has utilized Sotheby's catalogs of pre-Columbian artifacts in order to propose a framework for a bilateral agreement between Belize and the United States under the 1983 Convention on Cultural Property Implementation Act.[124]

While Davis's and Gilgan's works represent aspects of the market for antiquities in the West, they are not targeted toward quantifying the scale of actual looting in source countries. On the other hand, Ricardo Elia has examined a broader range of sources to understand the looting, sale, and collecting of Apulian Red-Figure vases from northern Italy.[125] In addition to quantifying the sale of these antiquities using market data, Elia relies on information from archaeological reports as well as publications from Italian law enforcement agencies to try to get a sense of the amount of looting, but he concludes that the true scale of looting might be impossible to determine using documentation alone. He concludes that thousands, if not tens of thousands, of tombs would have to have been looted to supply the number of known Apulian Red-Figure vases currently in worldwide collections.

The early China field can learn several things from these examples. First, while we are unlikely to be able to document the scale of looting using written testament and data alone, we might fruitfully comb site reports, which usually mention instances of previous looting, to calculate the number of sites impacted. The second thing we can learn from these examples is that market data are most useful for quantifying the consumption end of the illicit antiquities trade

---

[123] Tess Davis, "Supply and Demand: Exposing the Illicit Trade in Cambodian Antiquities through a Study of Sotheby's Auction House," *Crime, Law, and Social Change* 56.155 (2011), 155–174.

[124] Elizabeth Gilgan, 'Looting and the Market for Maya Objects: A Belizean Perspective,'" in Brodie et al., eds., *Trade in Illicit Antiquities*, 73–87.

[125] Ricardo J. Elia, "Analysis of the Looting, Selling, and Collecting of Apulian Red-Figure Vases: A Quantitative Approach," in Brodie et al., eds., *Trade in Illicit Antiquities*, 145–153.

network, specifically in identifying types of antiquities that fetch high prices and their likely origins. Given that the current memorandum of understanding between the United States and China covers artifacts dating from the Paleolithic period until the end of the Tang Dynasty (ca. 75,000 BCE–907 CE), as well as monumental sculptures more than 250 years old, more specificity as to what specific types of objects seem to be in most demand and in most frequent circulation might help advocates push for additional legislation, or at least give us an idea of what kinds of archaeological sites might need the most protecting.[126] Ideally, we should also do this kind of market analysis on the domestic consumption of Chinese antiquities to see how it compares with international demand. Today, many auction houses, such as China Guardian in Hong Kong, publish their auction catalogs as well as the results of their sales on their websites, so it might be straightforward to create a robust database of information regarding the kinds of objects for sale, whether they have provenances or proveniences, and whether they are in high demand compared to other types of objects.

Ultimately, choosing whether to engage with unprovenienced artifacts forces us to confront the intersection of historical, methodological, and ethical issues that exist in the field of archaeology, and Valmisa raises the important point that what really matters is how our decisions impact peoples' lives beyond the narrow realm of knowledge production, reception, and protection. To my mind, the issue comes down to how various interest groups value cultural heritage. Indeed, careful reading of most recent texts that address the issue reveals a common underlying theme of how the world values cultural heritage. For instance, Justin Jacobs's main argument is that it was possible for Western imperialists like Aurel Stein and Paul Pelliot to work with local communities in northwestern China to remove artifacts during the late Qing period and even into the early Republican period because each interest group involved, from Muslim laborers and guides to Confucian officials, benefited from the interaction based on their differential valuations of the antiquities.[127] Interestingly, Jacobs also argues that it only became difficult for these interactions to happen once two things occurred. First, the power of Western-trained Chinese scholars based in Beijing grew sufficient to disrupt the plunder; second, local northwestern communities, fueled by the growing sense of nationalism during the 1920s

---

[126] Memorandum of Understanding between the United States of America and China, 2019.

[127] Jacobs, *The Compensations of Plunder*, pp. 1–84. For other works that also have an underlying theme of cultural heritage value, see Haiming Yan, *World Heritage Craze in China: University Discourse, National Culture, and Local Memory* (New York: Berghahn Books, 2022), pp. 1–68; see also Shu-Li Wang and Michael Rowlands, "Making and Unmaking Cultural Heritage Value in China," in Jane Anderson and Haidy Geismer, eds., *The Routledge Companion to Cultural Property* (New York: Routledge, 2021), pp. 258–276.

and 1930s, became angry and mobilized against the removal of what they saw as their own cultural patrimony.[128]

Based on the evidence presented in this Element, it seems as though today, different stakeholder groups value Chinese cultural heritage in competing ways, from the Chinese state that sees cultural relics as symbols of national unity and political legitimacy, to Chinese archaeologists who, like international scholars, value artifacts for knowledge, but who also depend on cultural relics for their livelihoods to the point sometimes of needing to exploit them; from regular consumers for whom cultural heritage is entertainment, to collectors, who value art and antiquities as status symbols of personal prestige; and finally to the looters themselves, who value cultural heritage as a means of economic gain.

As a member of the scholarly community, I feel that the way researchers value cultural heritage, as knowledge-generating source material that should be accessible and beneficial as an education tool for everyone, ought to be the most prevalent valuation. I therefore also think that these values should be the foundation upon which policies and personal desires rest. Since this is the case, I come down on the side of using unprovenienced sources if we can be reasonably certain of their authenticity, and if the narrative a scholar wishes to write necessitates their inclusion. I do not necessarily adhere, however, to the idea that not using these sources does a disservice to scholarship because, as stated earlier and with reference to Valmisa's section of this Element, I believe there is room within the field to think more thoroughly about what kinds of narratives about early China we can and want to create.

In the same vein, I believe heritage stakeholders and interest groups should hold more open discussions about what value ought to be placed on cultural patrimony, and which stakeholder groups should take precedence in decision and rulemaking on the subject. The current situation in which looting takes place in China indicates that top-down legislation, with the state dictating the value of archaeological artifacts and immovable architecture, does not do enough to protect and preserve cultural heritage. Nor does international legislation like the 1970 UNESCO Convention, which serves mainly to limit looted objects from traveling across national borders. Additionally, the monetary value placed on antiquities, especially authenticated ones, as Goldin reminds us, continues to be a major problem that incites looting.

I believe that ideally, local communities in China who recognize the cultural patrimony in the environments around them should determine the value of cultural relics. This belief is influenced by Jacobs's arguments about the valuation of antiquities, by the work archaeologists have done to include descendent

---

[128] Jacobs, *The Compensations of Plunder*, 150–269.

communities at Sipan in Peru, and by Ko's emphasis that archaeology and cultural heritage can be collaborative processes rather than purely representative of either science or state.[129] Everything else, from administrative apparatuses to the advice and consultation of expert scholars both domestic and international, should serve to facilitate, guide, and carryout the wishes of those communities. I am not naïve enough to believe, however, that the monetary and symbolic values of antiquities held by collectors and states respectively, can simply be wished away, especially given how powerful entities like wealthy individuals, wealthy private institutions, and especially states are compared to scholars and local communities. Nor do I think it likely that scholars, especially international ones, have the power to immediately or quickly affect how these powerful individuals and institutions operate.

It is important that we, as scholars from outside of China, focus on positive engagement with local communities when we work with them through being transparent about our methods and intentions in our scholarship. We should also respect their need to use whatever land we are working on for their livelihoods, and try to advocate with and for them, so that as much as possible of the proceeds of the presentation and display of their cultural relics go back to their communities. Empowering local communities while advocating for changes to legislation and educating on the scholarly rather than monetary value of cultural heritage may be the next best actionable steps we can take.

---

[129] Ko states that, "The reconstruction of archaeological narratives-cum-heritage should then be made into a process representative of the participation of different immediate stakeholders rather than a fossilized product hegemonized by the ambitions of science and the state." Ko, "Remembering Qijiaping," 142.

3 Should We Use Unprovenienced Materials in Our Research? Epistemic, Methodological, and Ethical Issues (Mercedes Valmisa)

There are two sets of factors involved in our decision as scholars to use unprovenienced materials or refrain from using them in our research, where unprovenienced materials are defined as artifacts whose original location or find spot in an excavation is unknown.[130] The first set regards intrinsic factors involving issues pertaining to scholarship itself and the validity of these materials for the scholarship they produce. Intrinsic factors lead to epistemic and methodological issues. The second set regards extrinsic factors involving issues pertaining to the consequences of the study of these materials beyond academia itself and the scholarship it produces. Extrinsic factors lead to ethical issues.

The classification into intrinsic and extrinsic factors to assess our scholarly approaches to unprovenienced materials is useful for analytical purposes, but we must recognize that, as all divisions, it's not a fixed nor completely rigorous one. As Foster has remarked in our discussions, there is an ethical component to the first set of factors, namely a moral obligation to pursue responsible scholarship over reckless scholarship that could be damaging to the production of knowledge. There is also an epistemic component to the second set of factors, in that our ethical decisions eventually impact what data are available, lost, or prioritized.

With these caveats in mind, in my section of this Element, I separately present and assess both sets of factors, including tentative conclusions regarding the methodology and ethics of using unprovenienced materials in scholarly research. While the discussion regarding methodology is more narrowly focused on the Chinese case, as it addresses the specificity of the early Chinese textual corpus, the discussion on ethics is more broadly construed and could, in principle, be applied to unprovenienced materials from other civilizations.

Intrinsic Factors: Epistemic and Methodological Issues

A first important intrinsic factor leading to potential epistemic and methodological problems is that artifacts of unknown origins, as it is the case by definition with unprovenienced materials, may be forgeries. We rely on experts to authenticate unprovenienced materials and, as much as we may and should trust these authentication efforts, there is always a risk of error. Scholars working on unprovenienced materials that have been wrongly authenticated will produce false knowledge – that is, theories that appear valid but are based on false evidence and that may mislead scholarship for years to come. We could also

---

[130] "Unprovenienced" is to be differentiated from "unprovenanced," which refers to artifacts whose ownership history is unknown. Davis, "Supply and Demand," 163.

question authentication processes in terms of conflict of interests: a purchasing institution may have strong private interests in authenticating materials that have already been acquired.[131] While the risk of working in forged materials exists, a more pervasive problem is that, even if unprovenienced materials indeed are authentic, we have surely lost their archaeological context hence crucial data and evidence for identifying and interpreting them. For example, we don't know whether an acquired manuscript bundle is missing bamboo strips that the seller didn't retrieve or the buyer hasn't purchased, whether it was sitting near other texts or artifacts, who the owner or user of these artifacts was, what evidence for dating we are missing, so forth – a point both Foster and Chao also make.[132]

To further complicate the issue, Foster makes the relevant point that all excavation, whether by the hand of a trained archaeologist or by an untrained looter, is destructive – data are always lost. The question then becomes: what data are worth saving and what data can be sacrificed? The criteria looters use to make this decision are varied, though probably mostly economic. But let's not forget that archaeologists also approach digs with certain research questions in mind or a job at hand, such as salvage, that could be challenged from a different set of criteria.

I believe that both of these intrinsic problems (the risk of forgeries and the unavoidable loss of context and data) call for employing valid methodological practices rather than for the rejection of the materials. With regards to authentication, we must rely on professional expertise while advocating for transparency. If we are to trust experts' competency and institutions' interests in authenticating unprovenienced materials, we must demand transparency in communicating both the conditions of acquisition *and* the methods of authentication. Such transparency is not now enjoyed in the case of Chinese unprovenienced materials.[133] This information is key to understand the artifact that we are studying, and it may also help us establish trust (or distrust) in a particular artifact, cache, or institution. Of course, as Chao has further problematized in our discussions, we must also ask whose expertise is to be considered valid to settle an authentication case. Who is to be considered an expert? Is one expert's opinion enough or should decisions be reached by committee? But regardless how we answer these questions, most important is to demand and enforce transparent communication on standards, definitions, methods, and practices

---

[131] Chao and Foster also address the issue of conflict of interests in their sections of this Element.

[132] Chao discusses loss of context to raise interesting methodological concerns regarding Chinese archaeology's overreliance on typology.

[133] Goldin, "Heng Xian," 156. Foster proposes guidelines in Foster, "Introduction," 172. Goldin has recently published a new piece on this issue recapitulating his original argument and responding to his critics: Goldin, "The Problem," 145–151.

throughout the identification of materials of interest, purchase, and authentication processes.

I personally find the loss of context of discovery a more intellectually stimulating problem, especially with regards to reading Chinese manuscripts.[134] The fact remains that, even if a text has been authenticated by an institution and by experts who have transparently communicated the processes for acquisition and the methods of authentication (and which we deem worthy of trust), we may still find ourselves with a bundle of written bamboo strips whose order is unclear, which may contain two or more texts or be missing key sections, and so forth. We must treat this artifact as what it is: incomplete evidence. And we know that evidence lies at the heart of knowledge claims. In the traditional definition of knowledge, we need evidence to differentiate between *knowing* as the creation of justified true beliefs and simply guessing right by luck. Something becomes evidence for a belief when it enhances its likelihood, acceptability, or justification. In this light, we need the evidence that is missing from an unprovenienced text in order to justify any beliefs that we may form toward such text. For example, if we don't have evidence that the acquired materials represent a complete text, or that it's a single text as opposed to sections from two or more texts, it's difficult to justify reading the materials as a self-contained unity.

In light of this fundamental epistemic issue intrinsic to unprovenienced materials, how can we ensure the validity of these materials for the production of knowledge? Rather than rejecting unprovenienced materials as defective evidence, we must engage in appropriate methodological practices that account for their uncertain and potentially incomplete status. Crucially, I suggest that the validity of our scholarship in this case lies with identifying, acknowledging, and transparently communicating both the limitations and affordances of our materials, of the methodologies that we are employing in their study, as well as of our tentative results.

Before we can make newly found manuscripts publicly available, we must have recourse to philological, philosophical, historical, material, and literary arguments to reconstruct textual versions within available possibilities. As much as these reconstructions are fruitful in imagining possible texts that may have existed at a certain point in history and the connections that can be drawn between the new reconstructed text and the larger tradition, we are not justified to make any firm knowledge claims with regards to this text as an *ancient* or *historical text*. We can only make knowledge claims with regard to this text as

---

[134] As Foster has pointed out, while the focus of my discussion falls on the use of manuscripts for textual, literary, or philosophical analysis, there are other disciplines in which to study them, as well as many other unprovenienced objects to study besides manuscripts.

our creation, a well-informed reorganization of available materials within reasonable possibilities, which may result in a fictional text. However, that isn't a practice that I have ever seen in the Chinese or sinological academic contexts. Most commonly, scholars who work with reconstructed texts, including myself (whether it is their own reconstruction or the editorial team's), are interested in making knowledge claims regarding the acquired reconstructed text as a historical text, not as a newly created one. We engage in the reconstruction of the documents lost in transmission similarly to third-century poet Shu Xi 束皙, who, regretting that the Odes were not complete, proceeded to "fill them out."[135] Shu Xi did not see himself as *inventing* the lyrics of the lost ritual songs; he was *remembering* how they must have once been in accordance with the original intentions of the sages.[136] Is that how we envision ourselves in our engagement with the past? Do we aim at accurately reconstructing "how things were" or "should have been"? In her section of this Element, Chao follows up on this point by asking some crucial though challenging questions. Is it perhaps our time to start relinquishing the idea that the ultimate goal of scholarship consists in reconstructing a historically accurate past? Can we entertain new avenues of research that better fit the limitations of our sources, and, I'll add, that challenge a naïve realist conception of the past? Is there merit in accepting that our work is not a replication of the past but a responsible rewriting of new narratives?

I answer all these questions in the affirmative. Insofar as scholars are mostly interested in making knowledge claims with regards to the reconstructed text as an ancient or historical text (a text supposed to have existed at certain point in history), I argue contra Shu Xi that any claims must be articulated as purely speculative in the most traditional sense of speculation: as creative possibilities that may or may not be proven or falsified in the future depending on access to new evidence.[137] By virtue of lacking sufficient evidential support, one must

---

[135] As it reads in the Biographical Introduction to Shu Xi's rendition of the Odes, preserved in the *Wenxuan*: "[Shu Xi] often looked through the old Odes, regretting that they were not filled out, so he made poems to fill them out" 嘗覽古詩, 惜其不補, 故作詩以補之. Translation and context in Thomas J. Mazanec, "Righting, Riting, and Rewriting the *Book of Odes* (Shijing): On 'Filling Out the Missing Odes' by Shu Xi," *Chinese Literature: Essays, Articles, Reviews* 40 (2018), 5–32 (at 12–13).

[136] Many have shown that Chinese literati traditions often approached transmission different from Western ones – not necessarily as corruptive and implying loss but rather as opportunities to "correct" (*zheng* 正) or otherwise refine the texts, bringing them closer to a supposedly sagely original or adapting them to the new situational and contextual needs of changing times. See, among others, Susan Cherniack, "Book Culture and Textual Transmission in Sung China," *Harvard Journal of Asiatic Studies* 54.1 (1994), 5–125; Bruce Rusk, "Not Written in Stone: Ming Readers of the 'Great Learning' and the Impact of Forgery," *Harvard Journal of Asiatic Studies* 66.1 (2006), 189–231.

[137] My argument contra Shu Xi is playful, as we must understand that Shu Xi had crucial ritual, religious, and political reasons to incentivize and legitimize the filling out of the missing Odes. He was also operating within a very interesting horizon of hermeneutical possibilities and

suspend judgment regarding any definitive knowledge claim and propose hypotheses in a speculative manner. Jumping to conclusions (such as firmly establishing that reconstruction R represents an _original historical text_) is simply not reasonable in the face of insufficient evidence. Because we are missing key evidence to make judgments – for example, we cannot either verify or falsify the hypothesis that there are bamboo strips that have not been acquired – we cannot either confirm nor disconfirm, and hence there is no conclusive final judgment. Speculation is our only intellectual strategy to deal with this material by fruitfully putting to use all of our knowledge and skills – that is, paleographic, philological, historical, literary, philosophical, and so forth.

There are two important points to make regarding speculation as an intellectual strategy. The first is that speculation doesn't apply only to unprovenienced materials. Incomplete evidence characterizes much (if not all) knowledge. Nearly all inductive reasoning arrives at conclusions that go beyond existing evidence (unless the set of all evidence for an inductive claim can be proven to be all the evidence there is). And unprovenienced texts are not the only texts with partial, limited, or insufficient evidence. As pointed out earlier, scientifically excavated texts also experience loss and represent incomplete evidence. To different degrees, we encounter similar epistemic problems in the study of our received corpus too.[138] The second point is that, though we speculate because of lack of sufficient evidence, speculation isn't merely a second-class alternative for epistemic situations where a knowledge claim cannot be reasonably justified. Speculation is a fruitful exercise even in situations where crucial evidence is available – for example, archaeologically excavated manuscripts with a context of discovery (for which there is material evidence) and texts in the received tradition (for which there is historical evidence).

Pushing back against the evidence-first understanding of speculation in the sciences, Currie has recently proposed that speculative hypotheses not be judged in terms of evidential support, but on what he calls _productivity_: the wide range of epistemic benefits that a hypothesis might bring beyond its being well supported. In Currie's words, "A hypothesis is speculative when it aims to

---

creative composition in the late Han and Western Jin periods. See Mazanec, "Righting," p. 20; Mercedes Valmisa, "Wang Bi and the Hermeneutics of Actualization," in Albert Galvany ed., _The Craft of Oblivion: Aspects of Memory and Forgetting in Ancient China_ (Albany: State University of New York Press, 2023), pp. 245–267.

[138] For example, I don't have sufficient evidence to make knowledge claims regarding the contents of the received _Zhuangzi_ based upon the assumption that it was a closed text with clear structural divisions prior to its _date of compilation_ (third century CE). If I make claims based upon the assumption, say, that one section of the received _Zhuangzi_ already existed within a chapter in a closed text called the _Zhuangzi_ prior to Guo Xiang's edition (e.g. in the Warring States period), I am speculating and I surely should be transparent about the intellectual exercise that I'm performing.

be productive: its function is to provision epistemic goods through opening new research, or scaffolding the development of theories or experiments, or generating possibility proofs, or providing epistemic links to further knowledge."[139] Acknowledging the limitations of our research materials – importantly, not only the unprovenienced ones but virtually all of our materials to different degrees and extents – opens the doors to imagining new kinds of knowledge production that move beyond the attempt to reconstruct the past. The current pushback against evidence-first research could be put in dialogue with the legacies of the early twentieth century Doubting Antiquity (*yi gu* 疑古) movement in the broader context of challenging the foundations of the methodologies and epistemologies of early China studies.

I acknowledge that such challenges to a naïve realist reconstruction of the past may appear problematic to many, and that they may raise questions regarding the legitimacy of the scholarship based on such methodological praxes. A critic may ask, with Foster, in our speculative production of knowledge, whether there are any boundaries not to cross, some presumed historical anchors, some imagined ties back to the past through ambiguous transmission histories. For otherwise we could start composing our own texts à la *Zhuangzi* or as we presume that Confucius would have said (like many Chinese poets and philosophers have done before us). When does it stop being intellectual history or history of philosophy and it becomes our own contemporary literature, philosophy, or art *inspired* by Chinese sources? This valid concern should be assuaged by exploring, with Currie, some limiting conditions of productive speculation.

The first and most fundamental limiting condition, in Currie and Sterelny, claims that "speculation is a vice – is idle – when it is pointless: when it cannot or does not productively direct further inquiry; when it is not used to construct alternative scenarios to guide a search for evidence which would favour one at the expense of the other."[140] A second limiting condition is that speculation must be truth-directed, which I understand in connection with the condition that speculation not only generates new ideas but gives us the opportunity to link together our bodies of knowledge and generate new coherent narratives with them. As Currie notices, "the generation of narratives is often highly constrained by surrounding knowledge."[141] In this way, speculative generation of new narratives that deviate from the mainstream or traditional understanding of

---

[139] Adrian Currie, "Science and Speculation" *Erkenntnis* (2021), Springer online publication, https://doi.org/10.1007/s10670-020-00370-w.

[140] Adrian Currie and Kim Sterelny, "In Defence of Story-Telling," *Studies in History and Philosophy of Science Part A* 62 (2017), 14–21 (at 16).

[141] Currie, "Science and Speculation." On coherence, see also Currie and Sterelny, "In Defence of Story-Telling," 17–19.

an issue generates new "spaces of plausibility." Namely, speculative thinking makes room for new ways of determining how things hang together that weren't plausible under the norms, assumptions, and expectations of previous frameworks. For example, it's precisely the study of archaeologically excavated manuscripts that has persuaded many scholars that the interpretive framework in terms of authors-books-schools of thought is of limited and dubious applicability for the pre-imperial period. In this way, it becomes not only plausible but also fruitful to read early unprovenienced texts without the urge to assign them the label of, say, Confucian or Daoist, and to further generate a more general understanding of the intellectual and philosophical debates of the early period that isn't tied to divisions in schools of thought. But in order to generate these new spaces of plausibility, speculative narratives must be coherent with other existing bodies of knowledge (as for example, our current body of knowledge on early Chinese textual formation and textual practices).

A final limiting condition for speculative production of knowledge is that our hypotheses be presented *as speculative*, namely to be judged in terms of their *productivity* and not as a theory to be primarily judged on its evidential basis. Whether it is with unprovenienced manuscripts that have lost their "habitats" or contexts of discovery, scientifically excavated manuscripts whose strips have deteriorated over time and whose intended divisions and continuities are not self-evident, or with received texts for which evidence regarding authorship, contexts of creation, use, transmission, and circulation may be forever lost (unless new archaeological excavations bring it to light), the guiding methodological principle should be full transparency to ourselves and to our readers about our own working assumptions. The transparency in admitting a hypothesis as speculative shifts the aims of an investigation and the materials' affordances that may be identified and utilized for the production of knowledge.[142] Such transparency becomes even more of a methodological stepping stone to ensure the validity of our scholarship in the case of unprovenienced materials, where we face a radical lack of material and historical evidence to support our knowledge claims.

Extrinsic Factors: Ethical Issues

The second set of factors that we need to consider when making the decision whether to use unprovenienced materials in our research are extrinsic to scholarship itself insofar as they regard ethical issues that arise from the use of artifacts that may have been looted and trafficked. Problematizing the distinction that I establish between intrinsic and extrinsic sets of factors, Foster has

---

[142] Currie, "Science and Speculation."

pointed out that the intrinsic methodological issues previously discussed also carry ethical bearing for scholars. This is certainly the case, insofar as many scholars consider themselves obliged to abide by valid and appropriate methodological principles in their research (principles regarding transparency, charity, authenticity, etc.) due to our responsibility toward knowledge production. What I have characterized as intrinsic and extrinsic factors overlap in the sense of scholars' moral responsibility toward the creation of knowledge discussed in the previous section (intrinsic-methodological) and the protection of our cultural heritage that we discuss in this section (extrinsic-ethical). Nevertheless, there is an aspect of what I characterize as extrinsic factors leading to ethical issues that escapes the range of the methodological discussions previously raised: the extent to which our decisions as scholars may affect other people's lives *beyond* the realm of the production, reception, and protection of knowledge.

An important problem raised in this regard is that looting entails the destruction of our cultural heritage. Looters are rarely concerned with the conservation and protection of the past; whether due to lack of time, skill, expertise, or interest, they often destroy, lose, or misplace important data that professional archaeologists would have been capable to protect and conserve.[143] Renfrew and others have argued that the looting and its associated destruction of potential knowledge will continue unless museums and other purchasing institutions adopt regulations not to purchase unprovenienced artifacts, for the trafficking of antiquities, much as any other type of commerce, is a question of supply and demand.[144]

As long as there is a market for looted artifacts, there will be looters making a living thanks to this market. The question is to what extent scholars play a role in this market. Do we have the capacity to affect the unfolding of the looting market dynamics? Brodie, Renfrew, Goldin, and others have argued that scholars who use unprovenienced materials in their research indeed encourage further looting.[145] As long as scholars have an interest in and are willing to work with unprovenienced materials, institutions might have an incentive to continue purchasing looted artifacts. According to this view, we scholars are ultimately responsible for, or at least complicit with, the looting and the destruction of the

---

[143] Goldin, "Heng Xian," 156.

[144] Neil Brodie and Colin Renfrew, "Looting and the World's Archaeological Heritage: The Inadequate Response," *Annual Review Anthropology* 34 (2005), 343–361. Legal restrictions to protect the past and the world's cultural heritage are most efficacious when imposed in the countries where the purchasing of looted artifacts majorly takes place, rather than in the countries where looters are active. See Davis, "Supply and Demand."

[145] Goldin, "Heng Xian." Brodie and Renfrew, "Looting."

cultural heritage, as a representative sector within the target group of stake-holders who benefit from the trafficking of looted materials.

Foster has counterargued that, in weighing between two types of losses – the losses of the cultural heritage that will presumably continue to be suffered in the future by incentivizing looting and the losses we would suffer by neglecting looted artifacts that are already available – the second outweighs the first. He applies the concept of *rescuing* from salvage archaeology – salvaging what has been spoiled to preserve and learn from it as much as possible – and concludes that choosing not to study these materials would incur an act of destruction of knowledge comparable to the looters' act.[146] The morality of salvaging what has already been spoiled would be hard to deny if this were an isolated case. The problem is that, if we accept the hypothesis that the rescuing of looted artifacts leads to future lootings, salvaging creates an extended cycle of spoiled material and intellectual data in need of salvaging. Foster's argument could be qualified as conservative insofar as it accepts an inimical status quo (looting and destruc-tion of cultural heritage) and devises a strategy to minimize its harmful effects (rescuing) rather than proposing a solution to change the status quo (e.g., disincentivize looting). From an ethical perspective, an obvious objection to his argument would be to acknowledge that sometimes we need to accept a temporary harm, loss, or disadvantage, or forfeit goods, in order to enact change and enable a long-term collective benefit in the future. Some may argue that scholars must temporarily endure a partial loss of the cultural heritage and the knowledge production it affords in order to end looting and eventually be able to protect all of our cultural heritage.

That said, one may question the impact of scholarship on incentivizing the illegal market on antiquities, which in my view makes for a solid argument in favor of using unprovenienced materials in scholarly research. As Foster also remarks, there are many consumers of looted artifacts beyond researchers, such as galleries and private collectors, so the looting and the illegal market would certainly continue to flourish even if scholars did not study questionable artifacts. As Davis has argued with the market on Cambodian art, responsibility to regulate imports must lie with purchasing entities and countries, not with the country where the looting is taking place and much less with individual actors such as the final consumer, given the demonstrated unequal levels of impact or lack thereof between these parties.[147] Scholars are arguably the least

---

[146] Foster, "Introduction," 233.

[147] Davis, "Supply and Demand." New developments and recent revelations about the trade in this Cambodian material: Tom Mashberg and Graham Bowley, "Cambodia Says Its Found Its Lost Artifacts: In Gallery 249 at the MET." *New York Times*, August 18, 2022, www.nytimes.com/2022/08/18/arts/design/met-artifacts-cambodia.html.

responsible agents in incentivizing looting, where *responsible* is understood as having an obligation to do something due to one's actions having an impact on the course of events. There will always be buyers of looted artifacts and intermediaries and channels for looted artifacts to make their way into the hands of interested buyers of antiquities, even if scholars decided not to study these materials and even if countries and institutions imposed harsh regulations. The impact of scholars' research on unprovenienced materials is not proven, and it might be quite inconsequential, which is why Foster calls for devising better ways to measure our impact on looting, and to track changes in looting and damage to cultural heritage. Generating data and knowledge on these areas is imperative to inform our decision.

When a scholar decides to individually refrain from using unprovenienced materials, this must be understood as a demonstration of principles or a personal protest against what one may deem unethical or illicit activity. This is a legitimate individual choice of no consequence for the illegal market of antiquities. As ethical actors, we all continuously make compromises, choosing which principles to upheld and which ones to bracket. We may tolerate the exploitation of Chinese workers so that we can enjoy our iPhones and yet declare ourselves unable to bear the suffering of animals in factory farming and opt for veganism. When merely individual, these stances rarely have an impact beyond the person who thus chooses to live their life. And importantly, these personal choices cannot be elevated to universal ethical norms, since they may bring (unexpected and/or unintended) consequences that, evaluated from a different perspective or set of criteria, make the solution worse than the problem. Think, for example, of the research showing that plant-based food doesn't necessarily have a smaller environmental footprint, or the unintended but sometimes disastrous consequences of avoiding the purchase of certain products based on fair-trade criteria.[148]

Moreover, if the role of scholars incentivizing the trafficking of artifacts via their research in these materials is indeed marginal, Foster's salvaging argument gains renewed weight: in the face of the incapacity of our scholarly choices to stop the destruction of the cultural heritage, rescuing what has been spoiled certainly outweighs the intellectual benefits of holding a principled attitude. In this regard, a further argument in favor of studying unprovenienced manuscripts in particular is that specialized scholarly interests may incentivize the rescue and preservation of these ancient texts, which, without an academic market, probably wouldn't be salvaged in nonprofessional and illegal archaeological

---

[148] In his section of this Element, Foster explores the unintended consequences of rejecting scholarship on unprovenienced materials for early career scholars.

excavations, in favor of retrieving art objects, which enjoy a much larger and profitable market.[149] While our refraining from studying unprovenienced materials doesn't help the cause against looting, our studying them once authenticated in transparent ways does have a positive impact in the world. Given our current understanding of the dynamics of the looting market, it's clear that scholars should continue studying unprovenienced materials, but that doesn't mean that we shouldn't demand change at a different level.

Indeed, if people will always be interested in purchasing antiquities, there will always be looters. The most effective way to minimize the major negative effects of looting (the destruction of the cultural heritage) while not harming local economies is to regulate the extraction of material goods. If we want to end looting as the type of illegal and destructive activity that it is today all around the world, measures such as regulations at the level of purchasing laws, punitive measures against looters or buyers, or attempting to disincentivize looting by not studying unprovenienced materials are not enough. Governments must first activate the broken local economies that drive large numbers of people to earn their livelihood through risky and dangerous illegal activities.[150] As Foster also emphasizes, we need to understand the social realities that allow for looting.

There is something painfully hypocritical about placing blame in the looters as the perpetrators of a public harm that we academics and experts are responsible (and supposedly capable) to end. Looters are often the victims of corrupt and unequal socioeconomic systems, while they are just as legitimate inheritors of the past as we scholars are. In this regard, Zimmerman has noticed that, while archaeologists claim to act as stewards on behalf of the public, this *public* is far from homogeneous and may contain members who "have substantially different views of stewardship of the past than archaeologists."[151] We must ask the question *what public* we intend to benefit by stopping looting. Scarre cites the example of the Umatilla tribe, who thinks that the only way to treat their remains with respect is to rebury them, against archaeologists who want to retrieve them and store them in museums. The public also contains individuals and companies with socioeconomic interests such as building a school or a business in a site for the immediate and long-term benefit of the local community, which they judge to be more pressing and important than the preservation of the past.[152] Scarre

---

[149] See Foster, "Introduction."

[150] On the socioeconomic conditions that drive locals to loot tombs and the hardships of a life as tomb raider, see, among others, Hannah Beech, "Spirited Away," *Time* (October 13, 2003), https://content.time.com/time/world/article/0,8599,2056101,00.html.

[151] L. J. Zimmerman, "When Data Become People: Archaeological Ethics, Reburial, and the Past As Public Heritage," *International Journal of Cultural Property* 7.1 (1998), 69–86 (at 70).

[152] Geoffrey Scarre, "The Ethics of Digging," in Constantine Sandis, ed., *Cultural Heritage Ethics* (Cambridge: Open Book Publishers, 2016), 117–128.

calls our attention to the fact that it's difficult if not impossible to reconcile all interests. Even though he doesn't seem to be thinking about the looters themselves at all, aren't looters also legitimate part of the public? Aren't the interests and priorities that lead to looting also of legitimate concern when considering a broader public engagement with past remains? The harms and benefits of the local communities involved in looting must be central to our considerations, since we are dealing with their lives and the handling of cultural heritage to which they have the most immediate connection (e.g. their own ancestral tombs).

Why should looters not benefit from their inherited past in the way that they need to? What is our claim to ownership of the values that must be upheld and the ways in which the past must be put to use? We may claim that we have a responsibility toward the future humans who will inherit partial and spoiled knowledge because we failed to protect it. Don't we also, perhaps even more so due to the weight of actuality, have a responsibility toward living humans who are currently oppressed and need a way out of their situations?[153] If we are to demand something from governments of purchasing countries in order to avoid increasing numbers of people joining the business of looting, there's no reason to beat around the bush. Let's point to the socioeconomic conditions that encourage looting in local areas, and focus our efforts on the amelioration of these conditions for the people whose lives are therein intertwined. And let's offer viable alternatives for the communities that rely on looting to make a livelihood.[154]

Would we be willing to actually end looting without providing looters with an alternative career path in order to support their families? Reflecting on the illegal hunting and trafficking of African animals, Zimbabwean zoologist Muposhin complains that "Zimbabwe is on its knees because of economic

---

[153] On this point Foster questions whether all looters are poor locals looking for a means of livelihood hence sourcing to larger criminal networks. Would some looters participate in these activities as a hobby or for the thrill of it, inspired by popular culture that romanticizes looting? I respond with another question: what does it matter if *some* looters aren't financially compelled to engage in this line of work, as long as *most* looters participate in illegal extractions as a means of making a livelihood?

[154] As Beech has put it, "To see how locals are plundering their own heritage, travel to the desolate villages southeast of Xi'an, the city that is home to China's famed terra-cotta warriors. These villagers might be dirt-poor, but the earth is plenty rich" ("Spirited Away"). In 2001, an antiques dealer offered impoverished locals more than $60 for one night of work, about the same amount they earned in an entire year. As Beech remarks in the same article, the same is the case with many other desolate towns in Henan province near the city of Luoyang, the former capital of several historical dynasties, whose now poor peasant fields are littered with rich imperial tombs. Given an utter lack of opportunity to make a decent livelihood via legal and safer means, and partly due to the exorbitant taxation that has turned their farming unprofitable, locals in such communities all over China have adapted to become tomb raiders at different levels and scales (from one night shift to hereditary family businesses).

turndown, yet the international community expects our poor country to look after elephants and lions when we can't even feed our nation."[155] And he adds, "No one is coming to the table to say, 'Yes, we want you to stop this hunting, but here is a budget and an alternative plan you can follow instead.'"[156] In our case, such an alternative is the regulation of looters as *licit excavators of material goods*. It has been proven in different trafficking markets that prohibitions and penalizations work much less efficiently than regulations and legalizations.[157] Following with our parallel of the market of hunting and/or trafficking African animals (or parts of them, such as elephants' tusks), Namibia and Zimbabwe report better conservation and growing lion populations, respectively, as a result of regulating hunting as opposed to attempting to stop it altogether.[158] In African countries with regulated hunting, legal hunting provides "crucial benefits for rural communities and conservation."[159] Indeed, should hunting be completely halted, it's expected that Zimbabwe would lose a quarter of its elephant population.[160] Going back to looting, a regulated market of licit extraction of material goods, where looters become legal workers and there's access to basic conservation training could provide a crucial incentive for locals to protect archaeological sites in order to make a livelihood.

Mentioning the case of the Lord of Sipán excavation in Perú, in our discussions Chao remarked that one strategy archaeologists have employed to curb looting on the ground level is to bring local communities into the archaeological process with dedicated programs of education and training so locals have a deeper connection with archaeologists in their communities and develop a sense of duty toward preserving the finds in their lands. The Moche mummies (Lords of Sipán) excavation seems to have been fruitful in creating within the local community a sense of responsibility and ownership such that destruction through looting is deterred. Beyond building a sense of obligation toward the protection of a shared past, Foster remarks, locals must be given substantial financial incentives and a share in the profits and opportunities that legal archaeology brings to the community. More radically, in my view, looters themselves should be retrained, protected, and compensated as legal workers if we are to provide them with a legal professional alternative and fully

---

[155] Rachel Nuwer, "Hunt Elephants to Save Them? Some Countries See No Other Choice." *New York Times*, December 4, 2017, www.nytimes.com/2017/12/04/science/elephants-lions-africa-hunting.html.

[156] Ibid.

[157] The legalization, decriminalization, and depenalization of drugs is a paradigmatic example. See, among many other studies, Christopher Coyne, Christopher J. and Abigail R. Hall. "Four Decades and Counting: The Continued Failure of the War on Drugs." *Law & Society: Public Law – Crime* (2017); Joanne Csete et al., "Public Health and International Drug Policy: Report of the Johns Hopkins–*Lancet* Commission on Drug Policy and Health," *Lancet* 387 (2016), 1427–1480.

[158] Nuwer, "Hunt Elephants."   [159] Ibid.   [160] Ibid.

disincentivize the illegal extraction of material goods. There must ultimately be more benefit (not only necessarily financial, but *also* financial) in becoming a legal worker than in looting.

The *Shenzi* 慎子 already made this argument during the Warring States period (ca. fourth century BCE): if you want to get the best out of people, make them work for their own sakes, adapting to their needs, as opposed to forcing them to accommodate to yours. The relevant *Shenzi* passage reads:

> 天道因則大, 化則細。因也者, 因人之情也。人莫不自為也, 化而使之為
> 我, 則莫可得而用矣。是故先王見不受祿者不臣, 祿不厚者, 不與入難。
> 人不得其所以自為也, 則上不取用焉。故用人之自為, 不用人之為我, 則
> 莫不可得而用矣。此之謂因。

> The way of Heaven is such that those who adapt [to others] are great, and those who transform [others] are insignificant. Adapting means adapting to the dispositions of people. Humans all act for themselves. If I [attempt to] transform them and make them act for me, I will not be able to obtain and employ any of them. For this reason, the Former Kings did not employ as ministers those who would not accept a salary, and they did not undertake difficult projects together with those whose salary was not large enough. If people do not obtain what they need to act for themselves, those in power will not be able to make any use of them. Therefore, if you use what persons need to act for themselves, and do not use what make persons act for your own sake, there is nothing that you cannot obtain and employ. This is called adapting.[161]

If we want to prevent the harmful effects of looting, we need to provide an alternative to the many local communities that have adapted to rely on it to cope with their inimical socioeconomic conditions. By giving them an incentive to protect all of the archaeological past instead of destroying it while seeking for the most profitable pieces, we all win. Meanwhile, there is no substantial ethical reason scholars should collectively adopt as a norm not studying unprovenienced materials. Not studying these materials produces more harm than benefit, given that the incentive our research creates for reinforcing looting is so minimal within the complex and multilayered illicit art market. If we are concerned about the loss of cultural heritage and wish to have an impact on the development of the looting market, we scholars must think beyond purely scholarly choices and use our voices to recommend and instigate political actions.

---

[161] Shen Dao 慎到, *Shenzi* 慎子. Taipei: Shijie shuju, 1978, 2:3. On the ancient Chinese philosophy of *adapting*, see Mercedes Valmisa, *Adapting: A Chinese Philosophy of Action* (New York: Oxford University Press, 2021).

Bibliography

Alder, Christine, Duncan Chappell, and Kenneth Polk. "Perspectives on the Organisation and Control of the Illicit Traffic in Antiquities in South East Asia." Paper presented at Organised Crime in Art and Antiquities, Courmayeur Mont Blanc, Italy, December 12–14, 2009, 119–144. https://ro.uow.edu.au/lawpapers/76.

Alder, Christine, and Kenneth Polk. "Stopping This Awful Business: The Illicit Traffic in Antiquities Examined As a Criminal Market." *Art, Antiquity and Law* 7.1 (2002): 35–53.

Anhui daxue Han zi fazhan yu yingyong yanjiu zhongxin 安徽大學漢字發展與應用研究中心, Huang Dekuan 黃德寬, and Xu Zaiguo 徐在國, eds. *Anhui daxue cang Zhanguo zhujian* 安徽大學藏戰國竹簡. 2 vols. Shanghai: Zhonghua shuju, 2019–22.

Asano Yūichi 浅野裕一 and Ozawa Kenji 小沢賢二. *Sekkōdai saden shingikō* 浙江大左伝真偽考. Tokyo: Kyūkoshoin, 2013.

Baoli yishu bowuguan 保利藝術博物館, ed. *X Gong Xu: Da Yu Zhishui yu Wei Zheng yi de* ▢𬴊火公盨──大禹治水與爲政以德. Beijing: Xianzhuang, 2002.

Beech, Hannah. "Spirited Away." *Time.* October 13, 2003. https://content.time.com/time/world/article/0,8599,2056101,00.html.

Beijing daxue chutu wenxian yanjiusuo 北京大學出土文獻研究所, ed. *Beijing daxue cang Xi Han zhushu* 北京大學藏西漢竹書. 5 vols. Shanghai: Shanghai guji, 2012–15.

Brodie, Neil, Morag K., Christina L., and Katheryn W. T., eds. *Archaeology, Cultural Heritage, and the Antiquities Trade.* Gainesville: University of Florida Press, 2006.

Brodie, Neil, and Colin Renfrew. "Looting and the World's Archaeological Heritage: The Inadequate Response." *Annual Review of Anthropology* 34 (2005): 343–361.

Brodie, Neil, and Kathryn Walker Tubb, eds. *Illicit Antiquities: The Theft of Culture and the Extinction of Archaeology.* London: Routledge, 2002.

Brodie, Neil, et al., eds. *Trade in Illicit Antiquities: The Destruction of the World's Archaeological Heritage.* Cambridge: McDonald Institute of Archaeological Research, 2001.

Brown, Shana J. *Pastimes: From Art and Antiquarianism to Modern Chinese Historiography.* Honolulu: University of Hawaii Press, 2011.

Chang, K-C. "Chinese Archaeology since 1949." *Journal of Asian Studies* 36.4 (1977): 623–646.

Cherniack, Susan. "Book Culture and Textual Transmission in Sung China." *Harvard Journal of Asiatic Studies* 54.1 (1994): 5–125.

Cook, Constance A., and Paul R. Goldin, eds. *A Source Book of Ancient Chinese Bronze Inscriptions*. Revised Edition. Berkeley, CA: Society for the Study of Early China, 2020.

Coyne, Christopher, and Abigail R. Hall. "Four Decades and Counting: The Continued Failure of the War on Drugs." *Policy Analysis* 811 (2017): 14–21. https://www.cato.org/sites/cato.org/files/pubs/pdf/pa-811-updated.pdf.

Csete, Joanne et al. "Public Health and International Drug Policy: Report of the Johns Hopkins–*Lancet* Commission on Drug Policy and Health." *Lancet* 387 (2016): 1427–1480.

Currie, Adrian. "Science and Speculation." *Erkenntnis* 2021. Springer online publication. https://doi.org/10.1007/s10670-020-00370-w.

Currie, Adrian, and Kim Sterelny. "In Defence of Story-Telling." *Studies in History and Philosophy of Science Part A* 62 (2017): 14–21.

Davis, Tess. "Supply and Demand: Exposing the Illicit Trade in Cambodian Antiquities through a Study of Sotheby's Auction House." *Crime, Law, and Social Change* 56.155 (2011): 155–174.

Di, Yin Lu. "From Trash to Treasure: Salvage Archaeology in the People's Republic of China, 1951–1976." *Modern China* 42.4 (2016): 415–443.

Donnan, Christopher B. "Archaeology and Looting: Preserving the Record." *Science* February 1 (1991): 498–499.

Dutra, Michael L. "Sir, How Much Is That Ming Vase in the Window? Protecting Cultural Relics in the People's Republic of China." *Asian-Pacific Law & Policy Journal* 5 (2004): 62–100.

Elia, Ricardo J. "Analysis of the Looting, Selling, and Collecting of Apulian Red-Figure Vases: A Quantitative Approach." In Neil Brodie, Jenny Doole, and Colin Refrew, eds. *Trade in Illicit Antiquities: The Destruction of the World's Archaeological Heritage*. Cambridge: McDonald Institute for Archaeological Research, 2001, pp. 145–153.

Evasdottir, Erika E. S. *Obedient Autonomy: Chinese Intellectuals and the Achievement of Orderly Life*. Honolulu: University of Hawaii Press, 2004.

Falkenhausen, Lothar von. "Antiquarianism in East Asia: A Preliminary Overview." In Alain Schnapp, ed. *World Antiquarianism: Comparative Perspectives (Issues & Debates)*. Los Angeles, CA: Getty Research Institute Press, 2014, pp. 35–67.

Falkenhausen, Lothar von. "On the Historiographical Orientation of Chinese Archaeology." *Antiquity* 67 (1993): 839–849.

Falkenhausen, Lothar von. "Review of Yuri Pines, *Zhou History Unearthed.*" *Journal of Chinese Studies (Zhongguo wenhua yanjiusuo xuebao* 中國文化研究所學報) 73 (2021): 263–267.

Fischer, Paul. "Authentication Studies (辨文學) Methodology and the Polymorphous Text Paradigm." *Early China* 32 (2008–9): 1–43.

Fiskesjö, Magnus. "Bulldozing Culture: China's Systematic Destruction of Uyghur Heritage Reveals Genocidal Intent." *Cultural Property News.* June 23, 2021. https://culturalpropertynews.org/bulldozing-culture-chinas-systematic-destruction-of-uyghur-heritage-reveals-genocidal-intent.

Fiskesjö, Magnus. *China before China: Johan Gunnar Andersson, Ding Wenjiang, and the Discovery of China's Prehistory.* Stockholm: Museum of Far Eastern Antiquities, 2004.

Fiskesjö, Magnus. "Cultural Genocide Is the New Genocide." *Pen/Opp.* May 5, 2020. www.penopp.org/articles/cultural-genocide-new-genocide.

Fiskesjö, Magnus. "Politics of Cultural Heritage." In You-tien Hsing and Ching Kwan Lee, eds. *Reclaiming Chinese Society: The New Social Activism.* Abingdon: Routledge, 2010, pp. 225–245.

Fiskesjö, Magnus. "The Politics of Cultural Heritage." In You-tien Hsing and Ching Kwan Lee, eds. *Reclaiming Chinese Society: The New Social Activism.* New York: Routledge, 2010, pp. 225–245.

Fiskesjö, Magnus. "Rescuing the Empire: Chinese Nation-Building in the Twentieth Century." *European Journal of East Asian Studies* 5 (2006): 15–44.

Foster, Christopher J. "Further Considerations for the Authentication of the Peking University *Cang Jie pian*: With Brief Digression on the So-Called 'Han Board' Witness." *Early China* 44 (2021): 419–464.

Foster, Christopher J. "Introduction to the Peking University Han Bamboo Strips: On the Authentication and Study of Purchased Manuscripts." *Early China* 40 (2017): 167–239.

Friedrich, Michael. "Producing and Identifying Forgeries of Chinese Manuscripts." In Cécile Michel and Michael Friedrich, eds. *Fakes and Forgeries of Written Artefacts from Ancient Mesopotamia to Modern China.* Berlin: Walter de Gruyter, 2020, pp. 291–336.

Gilgan, Elizabeth. "Looting and the Market for Maya Objects: A Belizean Perspective." In Neil Brodie, Jenny Doole, and Colin Refrew, eds. *Trade in Illicit Antiquities: The Destruction of the World's Archaeological Heritage.* Cambridge: McDonald Institute for Archaeological Research, 2001, pp. 73–87.

Goldin, Paul R. "Heng Xian and the Problem of Studying Looted Artifacts." *Dao* 12 (2013): 152–160.

Goldin, Paul R. "The Problem of Looted Artifacts in Chinese Studies: A Rejoinder to Critics." *Dao* 22 (2023): 145–151.

Guojia wenwu ju 國家文物局. *Tianye kaogu gongzuo guicheng* 田野考古工作規程. Beijing: Wenwu chubanshe, 2009.

Guojia Wenwuju bian 國家文物局編, eds. *Disanci quanguo wenwu pucha baida xinfaxian* 第三次全國文物普查百大新發現 ("100 New Discoveries of the Third Nationwide Survey of Cultural Heritage"). Beijing 北京: Wenwu chubanshe 文物出版社, 2011.

Guojia Wenwuju bian 國家文物局編, eds. *2008 nian disanci quanguo wenwu pucha zhongyao xinfaxian* 2008年第三次全國文物普查重要新發現 ("Important Discoveries of the Third Nationwide Survey of Cultural Heritage, 2008"). Beijing 北京: Wenwu chubanshe 文物出版社, 2009.

Guojia wenwuju zhubian 國家文物局主編, eds. *Zhongguo wenwu dituji* 中國文物地圖集 ("Map of Cultural Relics in China"). Xi'an 西安: Xi'an ditu chubanshe 西安地圖出版社, 1989.

Guojia wenwuju zhubian 國家文物局主編, eds. *Zhongguo wenwu dituji: Hubei fence* 中國文物地圖集: 湖北分冊 ("Map of Cultural Relics in China: Volume on Hubei"). 2 vols. Xi'an 西安: Xi'an ditu chubanshe 西安地圖出版社, 2002.

He Shuzhong. "Illicit Excavation in Contemporary China." In Neil Brodie, Jennifer Doole, and Colin Renfrew, eds. *Trade in Illicit Antiquities: The Destruction of the World's Archaeological Heritage*. Cambridge: McDonald Institute for Archaeological Research, 2001, pp. 19–24.

Hein, Anke. "The Problem of Typology in Chinese Archaeology." *Early China* 39 (2016): 21–52.

Jacobs, Justin. "Confronting Indiana Jones: Chinese Nationalism, Historical Imperialism, and the Criminalization of Aurel Stein and the Raiders of Dunhuang, 1899–1944." In Sherman Cochran and Paul Pickowicz, eds. *China on the Margins*. Ithaca, NY: Cornell East Asia Program, 2010, pp. 65–90.

Jacobs, Justin. "Nationalist China's 'Great Game': Leveraging Foreign Explorers in Xinjiang, 1927–1935. *Journal of Asian Studies* 73.1 (2014): 43–64.

Kern, Martin. "'Xi Shuai' 蟋蟀 ('Cricket') and Its Consequences: Issues in Early Chinese Poetry and Textual Studies." *Early China* 42 (2019): 39–74.

Kirkpatrick, Sidney D., *Lords of Sipan: A Tale of Pre-Inca Tombs, Archaeology, and Crime*. New York: William Morrow and Company, 1992.

Ko, Jada. "Remembering Qijiaping, Forgetting Qijiaping: Archaeological Experience As Shared Heritage." *Bulletin of the Museum of Far Eastern Antiquities* 82 (2021): 135–180.

Lai, Guolong. "Digging Up China: Imperialism, Nationalism, and Regionalism in the Yinxu Excavation, 1928–1937." In Bonnie Effros and Guolong Lai, eds. *Unmasking Ideology in Imperial and Colonial Archaeology.* Berkeley: University of California Press, 2018, pp. 83–121.

Lai, Guolong. "The Emergence of 'Cultural Heritage' in Modern China: A Historical and Legal Perspective." In Akira Matsuda and Luisa Elena Mengoni, eds. *Reconsidering Cultural Heritage in East Asia.* London: Ubiquity Press, 2016, pp. 47–87.

Lazrus, Paula Kay, and Alex W. Barker, eds. *All the King's Horses: Essays on the Impact of Looting and the Illicit Antiquities Trade on Our Knowledge of the Past.* Washington, DC: SAA Press, 2012.

Li, Jian, Hui Fang, and Anne P. Underhill. "The History of Perception and Protection of Cultural Heritage in China." In Anne P Underhill and Lucy C. Salazar, eds. *Finding Solutions for Protecting and Sharing Archaeological Heritage Resources.* New York: Springer, 2015, pp. 1–16.

Liu Guozhong 劉國忠. *Zoujin Qinghua jian* 走近清華簡. Beijing: Gaodeng jiaoyu, 2011. [With English translation by Christopher J. Foster and William N. French as *Introduction to the Tsinghua Bamboo-Strip Manuscripts.* Leiden: Brill, 2015.]

Liu Huan 劉桓. *Xinjian Han du Cang Jie pian Shi pian jiaoshi* 新見漢牘蒼頡篇史篇校釋. Beijing: Zhonghua, 2019.

Ma Chengyuan 馬承源, ed. *Shanghai bowuguan cang Zhanguo Chu zhushu* 上海博物館藏戰國楚竹書. Shanghai: Shanghai guji, 2001–12, 9 vols. to date.

Mashberg, Tom, and Graham Bowley. "Cambodia Says Its Found Its Lost Artifacts: In Gallery 249 at the MET." *New York Times*, August 18, 2022. www.nytimes.com/2022/08/18/arts/design/met-artifacts-cambodia .html.

Maus, Amanda K. "Safeguarding China's Cultural History: Proposed Amendments to the 2002 Law on the Protection of Cultural Relics." *Pacific Rim Law & Policy Journal* 18.2 (2009): 405–431.

Mazanec, Thomas J. "Righting, Riting, and Rewriting the *Book of Odes* (Shijing): On 'Filling Out the Missing Odes' by Shu Xi." *Chinese Literature: Essays, Articles, Reviews* 40 (2018): 5–32.

Memorandum of Understanding between the United States of America and China, Signed at Beijing, January 10, 2019.

Meyer, Dirk. "Antiquity Resurfaced." Paper presented at Reading the Excavated Poetry (*Shijing*) from Early China: Perspectives from Paleography, Philology, Phonology, and Classical Exegesis, University of Notre Dame, October 26–28, 2018.

Miller, Peter N., and François Louis, eds. *Antiquarianism and Intellectual Life in Europe and China, 1500–1800*. Ann Arbor: University of Michigan Press, 2012.

Moser, Jeffrey. "The Ethics of Immutable Things: Interpreting Lü Dalin's Illustrated Investigations of Antiquity." *Harvard Journal of Asiatic Studies* 72.2 (2012): 259–293.

Moser, Jeffrey. "Why Cauldrons Come First: Taxonomic Transparency in the Earliest Chinese Antiquarian Catalogues." *Journal of Art Historiography*, no. 11 (2014): 1–23.

Murowchick, Robert E. "'Despoiled of the Garments of Her Civilization': Problems and Progress in Archaeological Heritage Management in China." In Anne P. Underhill, ed. *A Companion to Chinese Archaeology*. Hoboken, NJ: Wiley-Blackwell, 2013, pp. 13–34.

Murphy, J. David. *Plunder and Preservation: Cultural Property Law and Practice in the People's Republic of China*. Oxford: Oxford University Press, 1995.

Nuwer, Rachel. "Hunt Elephants to Save Them? Some Countries See No Other Choice." *New York Times*, December 4, 2017. www.nytimes.com/2017/12/04/science/elephants-lions-africa-hunting.html.

O'Connor, Francis V. "Authenticating the Attribution of Art: Connoisseurship and the Law in the Judging of Forgeries, Copies, and False Attributions." In Ronald D. Spencer, ed., *The Expert versus the Object: Judging Fakes and False Attributions in the Visual Arts*. Oxford: Oxford University Press, 2004, pp. 3–27.

O'Keefe, Patrick J. *Protecting Cultural Objects: Before and after 1970*. Crickadarn: Institute of Art and Law, 2017.

O'Keefe, Patrick J. *Trade in Antiquities: Reducing Destruction and Theft*. London: Archetype Publications and United Nations Educational Scientific and Cultural Organization, 1997.

People's Republic of China, State Council, Law of the People's Republic of China on the Protection of Cultural Relics, Adopted at Beijing, November 19, 1982.

Pines, Yuri. *Zhou History Unearthed: The Bamboo Manuscript Xinian and Early Chinese Historiography*. New York: Columbia University Press, 2020.

Poli, Maddalena. "Preparing One's Act: Performance Supports and the Question of Human Nature in Early China." PhD dissertation, University of Pennsylvania, 2022.

Qinghua daxue chutu wenxian yanjiu yu baohu zhongxin 清華大學出土文獻研究與保護中心, Li Xueqin 李學勤 (vols. 1–8), and Huang Dekuan 黃德寬 (vols. 9–12), eds. *Qinghua daxue cang Zhanguo zhujian* 清華大學藏戰國竹簡. Shanghai: Zhonghua shuju, 2010–22), 12 vols. to date.

Renfrew, Colin. *Loot, Legitimacy, and Ownership: The Ethical Crisis in Archaeology.* London: Duckworth, 2000.

Rusk, Bruce. "Not Written in Stone: Ming Readers of the 'Great Learning' and the Impact of Forgery." *Harvard Journal of Asiatic Studies* 66.1 (2006): 189–231.

Scarre, Geoffrey. "The Ethics of Digging." In Constantine Sandis, ed., *Cultural Heritage Ethics.* Cambridge: Open Book, 2016.

Sena, Yunchiahn C. *Bronze and Stone: The Cult of Antiquity in Song Dynasty China.* Seattle: University of Washington Press, 2019.

Senate and House of Representatives of the United States of America in Congress, Convention on Cultural Property Implementation Act, Public Law 100–204 [H.R. 1777], 101 Stat. 1331, Approved December 22, 1987.

Shaughnessy, Edward L. "General Preface II." In Edward L. Shaughnessy, ed., *The Tsinghua University Warring States Bamboo Manuscripts: Studies and Translations 1: The* Yi Zhou Shu *and Pseudo-*Yi Zhou Shu *Chapters.* Beijing: Qinghua daxue chubanshe, 2023, pp. 8–21.

Shen Dao 慎到, *Shenzi* 慎子. Taipei: Shijie shuju, 1978.

Smith, Adam. "The Ernest K. Smith Collection of Shang Divination Inscriptions at Columbia University and the Evidence for Scribal Training at Anyang." In Matthew Rutz and Morag M. Kersel, eds. *Archaeologies of Text: Archaeology, Technology, Ethics.* Oxford: Oxbow Books, 2014, pp. 121–141.

Smith, Adam, and Maddalena Poli. "Establishing the Text of the *Odes*: The Anhui University Bamboo Manuscript." *Bulletin of the School of Oriental and African Studies* 84.3 (2021): 515–557.

Smith, Corina. "'Authentic' *Venerated Documents*: What Are *Shu*, and What Is at Stake?" In Anke Hein and Christopher J. Foster, eds. *Understanding Authenticity in Chinese Cultural Heritage.* London: Routledge, 2023, pp. 221–234.

Stein, M. Aurel. *Sand-Buried Ruins of Khotan: Personal Narrative of a Journey of Archaeological and Geographical Exploration in Chinese Turkestan.* London: Hurst and Blackett, 1904.

Strong, Sarah, and Helen Wang. "Sir Aurel Stein's Medals at the Royal Geographical Society." In Helen Wang, ed. *Sir Aurel Stein, Colleagues and Collections.* British Museum Research Publication Number 184. London: British Museum, 2012, pp. 1–10.

Tong, Enzheng. "Thirty Years of Chinese Archaeology." In Philip L. Kohl and Clare Fawcett, eds. *Nationalism, Politics, and the Practice of Archaeology.* Cambridge: Cambridge University Press, 1995, pp. 177–197.

United Nations Education, Scientific and Cultural Organization. Convention on the Means of Prohibiting and Preventing Illicit Import, Export and

Ownership of Cultural Property, Adopted November 14, 1970, at the General Conference at Its Sixteenth Session, Paris.

Valmisa, Mercedes. *Adapting: A Chinese Philosophy of Action*. New York: Oxford University Press, 2021.

Valmisa, Mercedes. "Wang Bi and the Hermeneutics of Actualization." In Albert Galvany, ed. *The Craft of Oblivion: Aspects of Memory and Forgetting in Ancient China*. Albany: State University of New York Press, 2023, pp. 245–267.

Venture, Olivier. "Recently Excavated Inscriptions and Manuscripts (2008–2018)." *Early China* 44 (2021): 493–546.

Vitelli, Karen, ed. *Archaeological Ethics*. Walnut Creek, CA: Altamira Press, 1996.

Wang, Shu-Li, and Michael Rowlands. "Making and Unmaking Cultural Heritage Value in China." In Jane Anderson and Haidy Geismer, eds. *The Routledge Companion to Cultural Property*. New York: Routledge, 2021, pp. 258–276.

Wu, Hung. "Introduction." In Wu Hung, ed. *Reinventing the Past: Archaism and Antiquarianism in Chinese Art and Visual Culture*. Chicago, IL: University of Chicago Press, 2010, pp. 9–46.

Wylie, Alison. "Ethical Dilemmas in Archaeological Practice: Looting, Repatriation, Stewardship, and the (Trans)formation of Disciplinary Identity." *Perspectives on Science* 4.2 (1996): 154–194.

Yan, Haiming. *World Heritage Craze in China: University Discourse, National Culture, and Local Memory*. New York: Berghahn Books, 2022.

Zhang Chuanguan 張傳官. "Tantan xinjian mudu *Cang Jie pian* de xueshu jiazhi 談談新見木牘蒼頡篇的學術價值." *Chutu wenxian yu guwenzi yanjiu* 出土文獻與古文字研究 9 (2020): 329–358.

Zhang Zhongwei 張忠煒. "Chutu wenxian yanjiu de haiwai jingjian—ping *Xiguan Han ji: Xifang Hanxue chutu wenxian yanjiu gaiyao* 出土文獻研究的海外鏡鑒——評《西觀漢記: 西方漢學出土文獻研究概要》." *Guangmin ribao* 光民日報, 21 August 2019, plate 16. https://epaper.gmw.cn/gmrb/html/2019-08/21/nw.D110000gmrb_20190821_1-16.htm.

Zhuang, Min. "The Administration of China's Archaeological Heritage." In Henry Cleere, ed. *Archaeological Heritage Management in the Modern World*. London: Routledge, 1989, pp. 102–108.

Zimmerman, L. J. "When Data Become People: Archaeological Ethics, Reburial, and the Past As Public Heritage." *International Journal of Cultural Property* 7.1 (1998): 69–86.

Cambridge Elements ≡

Ancient East Asia

Erica Fox Brindley

Pennsylvania State University

Erica Fox Brindley is Professor and Head in the Department of Asian Studies at Pennsylvania State University. She is the author of three books, co-editor of several volumes, and the recipient of the ACLS Ryskamp Fellowship and Humboldt Fellowship. Her research focuses on the history of the self, knowledge, music, and identity in ancient China, as well as on the history of the Yue/Viet cultures from southern China and Vietnam.

Rowan Kimon Flad

Harvard University

Rowan Kimon Flad is the John E. Hudson Professor of Archaeology in the Department of Anthropology at Harvard University. He has authored two books and over 50 articles, edited several volumes, and served as editor of Asian Perspectives. His archaeological research focuses on economic and ritual activity, interregional interaction, and technological and environmental change, in the late Neolithic and early Bronze Ages of the Sichuan Basin and the Upper Yellow River valley regions of China.

About the Series

Elements in Ancient East Asia contains multi-disciplinary contributions focusing on the history and culture of East Asia in ancient times. Its framework extends beyond anachronistic, nation-based conceptions of the past, following instead the contours of Asian sub-regions and their interconnections with each other. Within the series there are five thematic groups: 'Sources', which includes excavated texts and other new sources of data; 'Environments', exploring interaction zones of ancient East Asia and long-distance connections; 'Institutions', including the state and its military; 'People', including family, gender, class, and the individual and 'Ideas', concerning religion and philosophy, as well as the arts and sciences. The series presents the latest findings and strikingly new perspectives on the ancient world in East Asia.

Cambridge Elements ⁼

Ancient East Asia

Elements in the Series

Violence and the Rise of Centralized States in East Asia
Mark Edward Lewis

Bronze Age Maritime and Warrior Dynamics in Island East Asia
Mark Hudson

Medicine and Healing in Ancient East Asia
Constance A. Cook

The Methods and Ethics of Researching Unprovenienced Artifacts from East Asia
Christopher J. Foster, Glenda Chao, and Mercedes Valmisa

A full series listing is available at: www.cambridge.org/ECTP

Printed in the United States
by Baker & Taylor Publisher Services